For my wife, Teresa, and my four kids, Courtney, Benjamin, Kenneth, and Andrew. Without them my life would not be as full and enriched as it has turned out to be.

Monterey Trail Runner's Guide

Jeffrey Van Middlebrook

WILDERNESS PRESS
BERKELEY, CA

FIRST EDITION APRIL 2001

Copyright © 2001 by Jeffrey Van Middlebrook
Edited by Paul Backhurst
Maps digitized by Jaan Hitt
Book and cover design by Jaan Hitt

Photographs by the author except where noted
Front and back cover photos: (top) Bluefish Cove from North Shore trail © 2001 by
Chuck Bancroft
(bottom) Sea Lion Point from Cypress Grove trail © 2001
by Chuck Bancroft
(back) Big Dome and Cypress Cove © 2001 by Chuck
Bancroft
Frontispiece: Jacks Peak with view of Point Lobos

Library of Congress Card Catalog Number 2001017721
ISBN 0-89997-281-0

Manufactured in Canada

Published by **Wilderness Press**
1200 5th Street
Berkeley, CA 94710
(800) 443-7227; FAX (510) 558-1696
mail@wildernesspress.com

Contact us for a free catalog
Visit our website at **www.wildernesspress.com**

Library of Congress Cataloging-In-Publication Data
Van Middlebrook, Jeffrey, 1949-
 Monterey trail runner's guide / Jeffrey Van Middlebrook.--1st ed.
  p. cm.
 Includes index.
 ISBN 0-89997-278-0
 Contents: Jacks Peak County Park -- Garland Ranch Regional Park -- Point Lobos State
Reserve -- Mission Trail Park.
 ISBN 0-89997281-0
  1. Running--California--Monterey Peninsula--Guidebooks. 2. Trails--California--Monterey
Peninsula--Guidebooks I. Title.

GV 1061.22.C2 V36 2001
796.42'5'0979476--dc21
  2001017721

Contents

Preface: **Running Philosophy**   vii

Using This Guide   1

Getting There   3

Weather and Seasonal Trail Conditions   6

Jacks Peak County Park   11
    Run 1: Nature Trail Loop   15
    Run 2: Earl Moser Trail Loop   19
    Run 3: West-end Lower Fire Road Loop   23
    Run 4: West Lot to East Lot Loop   27
    Run 5: Great Inner Loop   31
    Run 6: Great Outer Loop   35

Garland Ranch Regional Park   39
    Run 7: River Floodplain Loop   41
    Run 8: Upper Mesa Loop   45

Point Lobos State Reserve   50
    Run 9: South 1-Mile Loop   53
    Run 10: North 2-Mile Loop   55
    Run 11: Whalers Knoll Loop   59
    Run 12: South Inner Forest Loop   63
    Run 13: Outer 3.5-Mile Loop   68
    Run 14: Big Outer Loop   74

Mission Trail Park   81

Run 15: Lower Gate to Upper Bridge (& back)   85
Run 16: Upper Bridge (& back) via Willow Trail   87
Run 17: Eastside Switchback Route   89

Afterword   92

Acknowledgments   93

About the Author   95

Index   96

Preface

Running Philosophy

THE SOLE OBJECTIVE OF THIS GUIDE IS TO GET PEOPLE OFF PAVE-MENT, AWAY FROM CARS, AND OUT INTO THE MEDITATIVE SOLITUDE AND BEAUTY OF MONTEREY PENINSULA FORESTS. UNLIKE MY ORIGINAL 1978 guide that had as many paved runs as it did trail runs, and my 1993 update that also had a few paved runs, this book focuses solely on unpaved trail runs. Any pavement crossed in order to connect trail segments amounts to only a few yards at most.

My obsession with unpaved routes is the natural evolution of over 30 years of running. Approaching my 50th year, I've learned that my feet, ankles, and joints cannot take the continual impact imposed on pavement. If I totaled my mileage over the last three decades, I could probably have circumnavigated the globe. About two thirds of that mileage was on pavement for much of the first two decades. As a competitive runner during those years, my body took a terrible pounding. Is it any wonder that I'd often quit for months at a time due to injuries and runner's burn-out, resulting from the stress of running on hard pavement and watching my watch?

Having developed a healthy attitude about running and what it can and cannot do, I dedicate this guide to those in transition (even if unaware of it now) to an enlightened awareness in running. I cannot prevent obsessed, competitive runners from using it, but it hasn't been written for them. Running should be an experience that helps a person achieve a higher level of health and fitness, while simultaneously exciting the senses and enriching the soul. Because running cannot prevent old age, disease, and death, running only to compete becomes a game of diminishing returns. Yet that's how it is market-ed. Too many people run for the wrong reasons. Neither a timed dirge nor an impossible quest, running should be a lifting joy. While anyone can benefit from the incredible workouts described here, developing an appreciation for trail aesthetics takes you to another level. Use this guide to become the sort of runner who runs for pleasure. Trail running will set the stage for the possibility of change.

"

If you run for the right

reasons, it adds quality to your life

—not to mention longevity. **"**

Using This Guide

EACH CHAPTER FOCUSES ON ONE PARTICU-
LAR TRAIL VENUE. EACH VENUE IS EITHER
A STATE, COUNTY, OR CITY PARK SET ASIDE AS
an "urban wilderness" where a network of
trails has been established. Each chapter's
opening page has a map of the location of the
run. Text on the facing page briefly describes
what sort of aesthetics to expect, the range of
difficulty of the runs, and other facts and
comments.

Following the chapter's opening pages
are the map and text for each run. Though
otherwise a duplicate of the location map, the
specific run being described is highlighted
here. The text covers how to find the trailhead
for the run, how to stay on route, difficulty of
the run, round-trip mileage, and other pertinent data. Difficulty ratings are indicated by
the following icons:

Easy 👟
Moderate 👟👟
Strenuous 👟👟👟
Very Strenuous 👟👟👟👟

Subsequent runs in a particular venue
can incorporate—either a part or the whole

1

of—earlier, shorter runs to create uniquely different routes. So read each description in your chosen venue consecutively, and perhaps run them consecutively, to familiarize yourself with all the routes. Several on-site trials can be necessary before you master some of them. But that's part of the fun and adventure in trail running.

Areas Omitted

Even when running along the ocean's shore it's difficult to stay in a meditative state of mind if cars are omnipresent and your body is responding to continual pavement pounding. I have chosen to exclude any paved runs from this guide and, sadly, Pacific Grove offers no "wilderness" trails. While there is a system of connecting trails along Pacific Grove's 6-mile-long shoreline that I frequently run, I've omitted it because of ever-present automobile sights and sounds. Carmel does offer a very fine "wilderness" trail system, included in this guide, but its brief shoreline trail has been excluded for the same reason as Pacific Grove's. Pebble Beach offers nice trails with plenty of solitude but all of the undeveloped land within Pebble Beach boundaries (often referred to by locals as the Del Monte Forest) is private. Though I have run these trails and mountain bikers use them, the Pebble Beach Company, which administers that domain, reserves the right to determine access. Without knowing their official position regarding trail use, I've chosen to exclude coverage of these trails from this guide.

Getting There

Though there can be several ways to get to some of the book's venues, to simplify matters I'm providing one preferred route.

JACKS PEAK PARK: TAKE THE OLMSTED ROAD TURNOFF FROM HIGHWAY 68 OPPOSITE THE MONTEREY AIRPORT ENTRANCE. OLMSTED Road heads south past open fields and an elementary school on the right. After winding up a gentle slope, the road first levels off and then drops to a prominent curving dip in the road. At the low point of this dip is the gated turnoff to Jacks Peak Park. The kiosk entrance (beyond the second gate) is staffed only on weekends. During the week you're on the "honor system" to pay the nominal fee by envelope. While drive-in access hours are from 11:00 A.M. to 7:00 P.M. daily, walk-in or run-in access is unlimited.

Garland Ranch Park: Take Carmel Valley Road 12 miles east from Highway 1 to the obvious dirt parking lot for Garland Ranch Park, on the right of a right-sweeping curve alongside the Carmel River. There is no parking or access fee for Garland Ranch Park and access hours are unlimited.

Point Lobos State Reserve: Drive 3 miles south of Carmel Valley Road on Highway 1 to the well-marked entrance for Point Lobos. While there is a drive-in fee every day of the year, if you arrive early enough or late enough you can park on the east side of Highway 1 just outside, and walk/run in for free. Hours of access are from 9:00 A.M. to 5:00 P.M. during winter, 9:00 A.M. to 7:00 P.M. in summer. All access—by car or on foot—is limited to these hours.

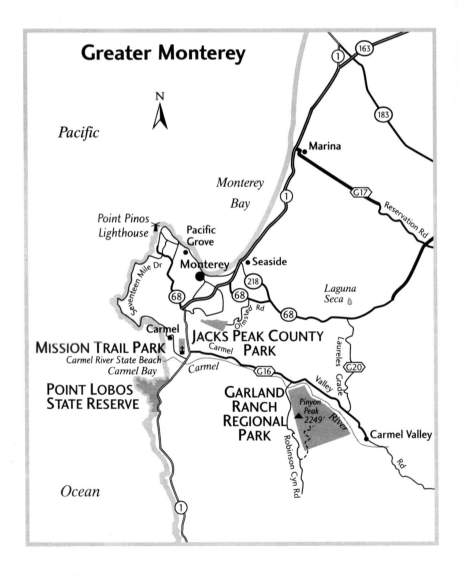

Greater Monterey

N

Pacific

Monterey
Bay

Marina

Point Pinos
Lighthouse

Pacific
Grove

Seventeen Mile Dr

Monterey

Seaside

218

Laguna
Seca

68

68

Olmsted Rd

68

Carmel

JACKS PEAK COUNTY
PARK

MISSION TRAIL PARK
Carmel River State Beach
Carmel Bay

Carmel

Carmel

POINT LOBOS
STATE RESERVE

G16

GARLAND
RANCH
REGIONAL
PARK

Pinyon
Peak
2249'

Laureles Grade

G20

Valley

River

Carmel Valley

Robinson Cyn Rd

Rd

Ocean

1

G17

Reservation Rd

1   163

183

Mission Trail Park: Drive less than a mile west on Rio Road from Highway 1, until you see the Carmel Mission straight ahead. To your left are baseball fields. Immediately past the turnoff to a parking lot, is the southern entrance for Mission Trail Park on your right. You will see a dirt road behind a locked steel gate, with a wooden sign on the right designating the park. Leave your car on either side of Rio Road, or park in the baseball-field parking lot. There's no entrance fee, and hours of access are unlimited.

There is limited public transportation available to these venues via the Monterey-Salinas Transit (MST) bus system. If you want to use the MST system, contact them for a current schedule at: (831) 899-2555.

Weather and Seasonal Trail Conditions

MONTEREY PENINSULA LOCALS ARE FOND OF SAYING THAT WE HAVE TWO SEASONS: FOGGY AND RAINY. THOUGH NEITHER WHOLLY true nor completely false, it's true that the Monterey area gets a great deal of fog—mostly during the summer. A few years ago a new record for consecutive days of fog (never seeing the sun once) was set in the month of August: 31 days out of 31 days! Such persistent fog tends to have a corrosive effect on a person's mood and behavior as attested to by locals. But for trail runners fog can be an ally.

This guide covers four locales, with terrain ranging from heavily wooded with some hills to very hilly. It can be taxing to run these trails on a hot day. Fog provides two significant advantages for the trail runner: its cool, damp atmosphere makes running easier and limits the number of tourists on the trails. This latter advantage is obvious at Point Lobos State Reserve. When the weather is clear, sunny, and warm, tourists swarm Point Lobos. Yet on cold, foggy days, I've enjoyed numerous runs and never seen another soul. And there is nothing quite like running alone in the woods with fog commingling with the pines!

Monterey's rainy season tends to be restricted to the winter months and storms are quite sporadic. In years of heavy rainfall most of the trails described here become muddy and flooded and suffer minor washouts. While the integrity of the trails' surfaces is never a concern, flooded trails can be unsafe for you to run. Determine conditions before you set off.

One natural threat found in Monterey's park areas is from falling trees and tree debris. The Monterey pine (*Pinus radiata*) has a very shallow root system and grows relatively fast, reaching old age within 40–60 years. These factors make for brittle wood and unstable footing. While the coastal live oak (*Quercus agrifolia*), a notoriously tough tree that rarely falls over even during severe windstorms, dominates at Garland Ranch Park, the Monterey pine is the dominant tree at three of the four parks listed in this guide: Point Lobos, Jacks Peak, and Mission Trail. Since these pines are highly susceptible to high winds, you commonly encounter fallen trees at these three locations. The incidence of falling pines increases greatly when high winds are joined by heavy rains. Rain loosens already precarious rootholds and wind then topples the trees with relative ease. While running at these venues, I have sometimes witnessed large pines

Cypress Grove Loop at Point Lobos

crashing down. On occasion I've had to cut a run short during wind- and rainstorms because the amount of life-threatening debris crashing down out of towering pines has created the equivalent of Mother Nature's war zone. While it adds an unexpected thrill to the run, the idea is to enjoy life, not lose it prematurely!

The Monterey area's best seasons for fog- and rain-free weather are spring and fall. September and October, when we have our Indian summer, bring the hottest weather. Jacks Peak and Garland Ranch parks, farther from the coast, are the two running venues here that have less impact from the fog.

"

Run without wearing a watch. Your body is the best clock to tell you how fast you should be going and when it's time to stop. **"**

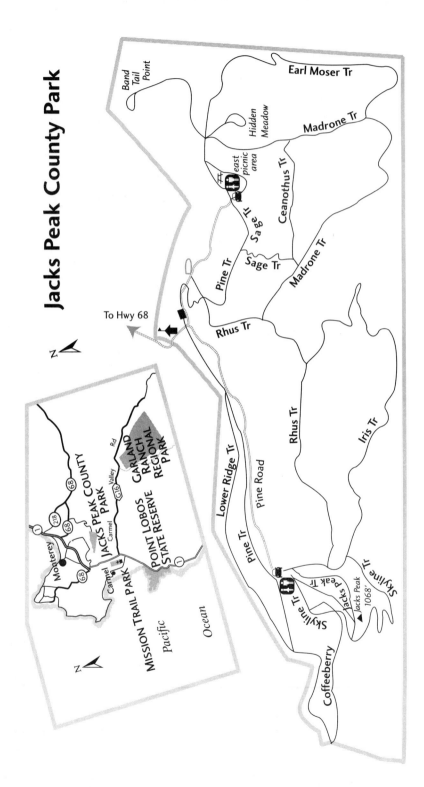

Jacks Peak County Park

Jacks Peak
County Park

JACKS PEAK PARK IS MONTEREY'S BEST KEPT
SECRET. WHILE NOT THAT BIG IN TERMS OF
SQUARE MILES, THIS FORESTED PARK STRADDLES
a prominent ridgeline separating the cities of
Monterey Bay to the north from Carmel
Valley to the south. Given its rugged, undulat-
ing terrain and network of interconnecting
trails, Jacks Peak Park offers the serious trail
runner a wonderful choice of routes.

The route distances range from exactly 1
mile to over 6 miles. The range of difficulty is
as varied, from relatively easy uphills to steep
and gruelling stretches that tax even the
strongest runner.

Although there are challenges in distance
and difficulty, every run at Jacks Peak Park
affords the runner great views of Monterey
Bay and/or Carmel Valley. And, on even the
most popular hiking trail loop, solitude is almost guaranteed because so few people avail
themselves of this park.

Because this park is grossly underused,
you should consider some potential risks.
Cougars are known to live here, and I encountered one during a run in 1992. Based upon

Hill climb on natural loop

what I've been told since, I suppose I'm lucky to be alive, even though human kills by cougars are rare. But that was one encounter out of literally hundreds of times I've run there. You're unlikely to encounter a cougar, but the possibility exists. For this reason you may choose to run with a partner, or carry pepper spray as I do now. However, the spray may engender a false sense of security rather than act as an objective deterrent to an attack.

The other factor to consider—especially if you are a woman—is that the park trails' remoteness coupled with their very little use poses the possibility of an assault by humans. I've been hassled twice by gangs who've gone there during school hours to hang out. Again, this is a rare occurrence but it can happen.

The purpose of this discussion is not to deter the trail runner from using Jacks Peak Park. To the contrary, I encourage you to go there, for you will not regret the experience. But I would be remiss not to inform the interested runner of those safety factors to consider.

"

Look around you while you run.

Smell the aromas of the earth.

Listen to the sounds of nature.

Enjoy the sun and the wind against

your skin. Running should invigorate

all the senses. **"**

Jacks Peak County Park

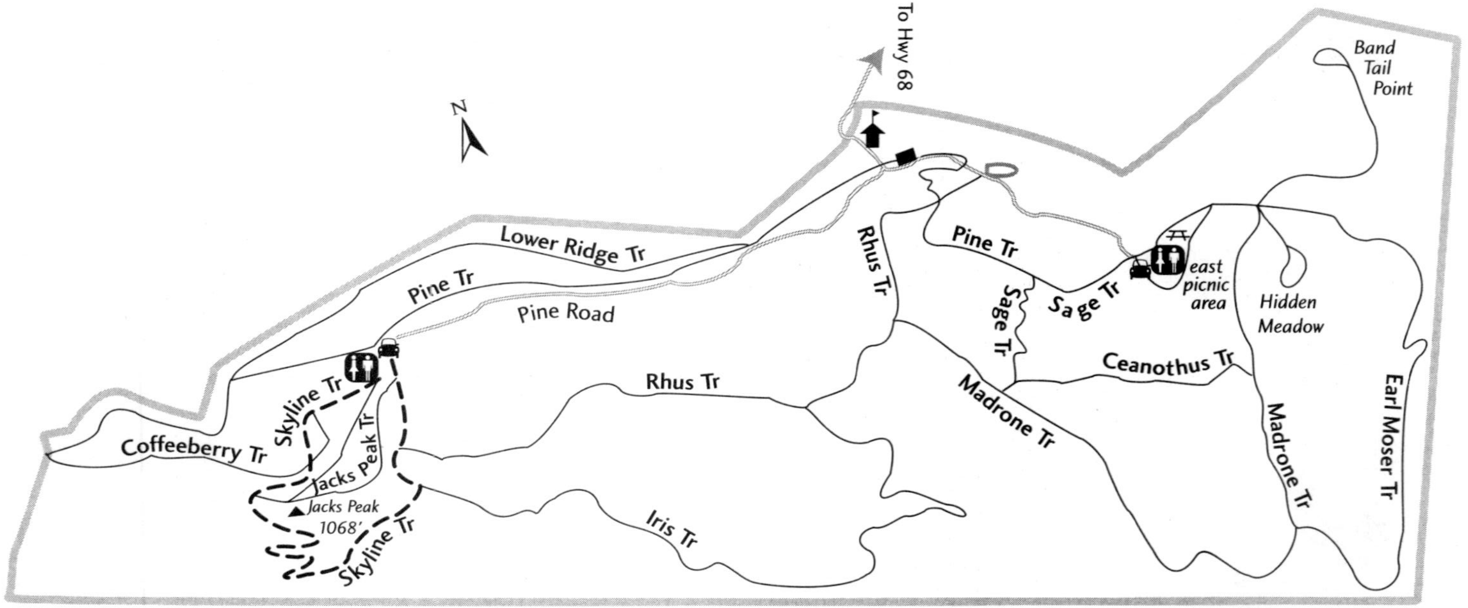

Band Tail Point

Earl Moser Tr

Hidden Meadow

Madrone Tr

east picnic area

Ceanothus Tr

Sage Tr

Sage Tr

Madrone Tr

Pine Tr

To Hwy 68

Rhus Tr

Rhus Tr

Iris Tr

Lower Ridge Tr

Pine Road

N

Pine Tr

Jacks Peak Tr

Skyline Tr

Jacks Peak
1068'

Skyline Tr

Coffeeberry Tr

Nature Trail Loop

Distance: 1 mile   Difficulty: 👟👟

Perhaps the prettiest little run at Jacks Peak Park, this trail loop is one of the best runs in this guide.* This route is only a 1-mile loop but it offers everything: hard hills, nice downhills for recovery, fantastic views, and a lot of natural beauty. I use it to run laps, alternating directions with each lap. If I'm feeling especially energetic, I will do as many as eight laps for a fantastic workout.

Getting to the trailhead is as simple as turning right just beyond the entrance kiosk and driving to road's end at the west parking lot. Near the bathroom building on the lot's north side is a display case that has pertinent park information posted and maps. The trailhead is directly left and uphill from this case.

If you choose to start this loop from the trailhead noted above, your first 100 yards will be a steep uphill climb past a water tank left of the trail. Just after you pass it the trail levels and you come to a bench, which offers a view of Monterey Bay. This is the first of four benches that you pass on this loop. Of these, three are named and dedicated to individuals. The unnamed bench is just three split logs assembled in a semicircle beneath a large Monterey pine, but it provides a commanding view southwest of Point Lobos State Reserve and the Pacific Ocean.

My pick for the best runs are Jacks Peak #1, Jacks Peak #2, Jacks Peak #4, Point Lobos #13, Point Lobos #14, and Point Lobos #11, not necessarily in that order.

The "kissing trees" on the Nature Trail Loop

Just past the first bench the trail climbs again briefly, then descends for 100 yards to a trail junction. The left branch goes to a historical marker. The right branch, named the *Coffeeberry Trail*, descends for a half mile to a gate and a dead-end public road. Go straight ahead. Just past this trail junction the loop curves right and you pass another display case containing fossil rocks on the left.

This loop continues on a pleasant level for another 100 yards. It then climbs briefly and steeply to another trail junction. The left fork goes to the official summit of Jacks Peak. Take the right fork, which immediately descends crude steps, at the bottom of which you should take a sharp left. Within a short, level distance you come to a second bench, the split-log bench. Just beyond it the trail begins a long descent, which includes several switchbacks.

At the bottom of the switchbacks is the third bench; then the trail briefly levels out before beginning an easy climb along a brushy hillside. After this section tops out, the trail roller-coasters for a couple of hundred yards. The Monterey pine and coastal live oak seem entwined in an embrace along this section of trail, and I call them the "kissing trees." This trail section also contains the fourth and last bench, which my kids nicknamed "Grandpa's bench" because it's dedicated to the memory of their maternal grandfather, Hugh Benjamin Fife. It was the last privately dedicated bench permitted in Jacks Peak Park.

Shortly after passing this last bench you reach another trail junction. The trail route for *Run 6* descends to the right. Take the left fork. After you top out on a short, steep climb, you drop for a nice long, level run, soon reaching another junction. Keep straight ahead. The trail emerges from forest cover and begins a gentle uphill climb back to the parking lot.

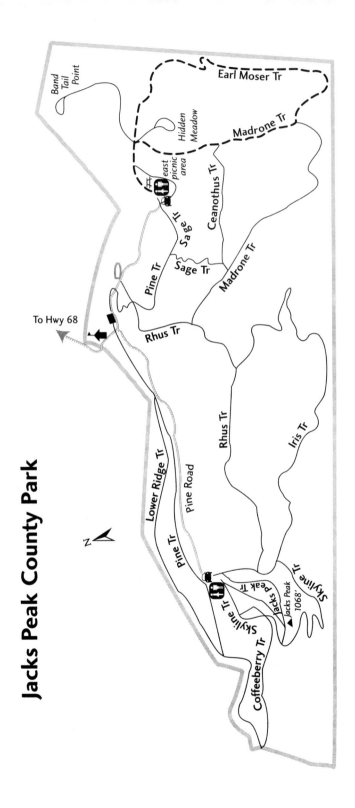

Jacks Peak County Park

Band Tail Point

Earl Moser Tr

Hidden Meadow

Madrone Tr

east picnic area

Sage Tr

Sage Tr

Ceanothus Tr

Madrone Tr

Pine Tr

To Hwy 68

Rhus Tr

Rhus Tr

Iris Tr

N

Lower Ridge Tr

Pine Road

Pine Tr

Skyline Tr

Jacks Peak Tr

Jacks Peak 1068'

Skyline Tr

Coffeeberry Tr

Earl Moser Trail Loop

Distance: 2 miles   Difficulty: 👟👟👟

This east-end loop is one tough little run! It's named in honor of a man who was involved with the local chapter of the Sierra Club for many years and was instrumental in the creation of Jacks Peak Park.

To reach the *Earl Moser Trail*, turn left just past the entrance kiosk and drive to the road's end at the east parking lot. South of the lot is a bathroom building. While the loop could begin at three different points, if you look north of the lot, away from the bathroom, you will see a sign designating the start of the *Earl Moser Trail*.

For 100 yards the trail dips past the BBQ/picnic area, then it climbs briefly to a junction. Continuing straight ahead you soon drop steeply down a fire road to a five-way junction. The hard right fork (fire road) offers a steep descent, which is the shared route of more than one run in this guide. The other right fork—at less of an angle—is a road that leads to a dead end. So does the left fork. Straight ahead a wooden sign confirms you're on the *Earl Moser Trail.*

The trail now begins a long steep climb with switchbacks here and there—a calf-burner! Almost relentlessly uphill for a good half mile, the trail has only a few, brief level and downhill stretches to allow you some recovery. But the "burn" is worth the effort, because once the trail levels off you are treated to a long cruise through pines and meadows, across a mesa-like ridgetop.

Along this ridgetop you pass a bench on the right side of the trail. Not far beyond it the trail begins its descent. Left of the trail you

19

see a barbed-wire fence that marks the boundary between public and private lands. Beyond this fence are deer trails that could take the adventurous down to Carmel Valley Road after many miles. Some of them traverse Clint Eastwood's land developments, including custom homes and a new golf course.

The trail soon comes to a steep downhill set of steps with a railing. At the bottom of these steps a road descends steeply to a junction with the aforementioned fire road. Turn right and stay on this road. It climbs gently for a half mile, and then climbs steeply back up to the five-way junction. Take the left fork, which climbs steeply back up to the point where you'll see the east parking lot.

Summit Meadow on the Earl Moser Loop

Jacks Peak County Park

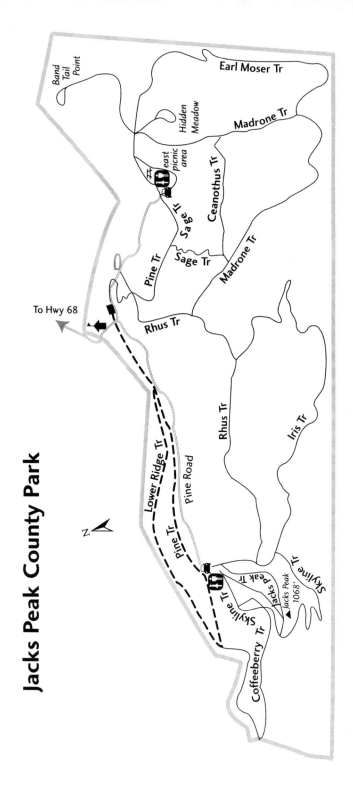

Band Tail Point

Earl Moser Tr

Hidden Meadow

Madrone Tr

east picnic area

Ceanothus Tr

Sage Tr

Sage Tr

Madrone Tr

Pine Tr

To Hwy 68

Rhus Tr

Rhus Tr

Iris Tr

Lower Ridge Tr

Pine Road

Pine Tr

N

Skyline Tr

Jacks Peak Tr

Jacks Peak 1068'

Skyline Tr

Skyline Tr

Coffeeberry Tr

West-end Lower Fire Road Loop

Distance: 2 Miles   Difficulty: 👟

While this loop is probably the easiest run at Jacks Peak covered in this guide, it is a beautiful route entirely worthy of your running.

It was here that I encountered a cougar in 1992. I made a split-second decision to keep running toward the cougar, hoping the cat would interpret my boldness as an aggressive threat. The strategy worked as the cougar began running away from me, eventually bolting off the trail after about a hundred yards.

After turning right past the entrance kiosk and driving to the west parking lot, you can find the start of this route just behind the bathroom building.

For the first quarter mile you drop rapidly down a steep fire road to a junction with another fire road. Turn right and cruise for just over another quarter mile along a gentle downgrade. Shortly after this road levels off, it begins a long, gentle upward climb to a steel-pole gate where the fire road merges with the paved main road (heading to the west parking lot). The trail continues just left of the gate. The trail now climbs steeply for 100 yards and then levels off for another 100. After that it drops quickly down to the entrance kiosk.

The kiosk is the turnaround point for this route. Retrace your steps along the same trail to the steel gate. Instead of turning right to head back along the fire road, continue straight ahead, parallel to the gate, and pick up a trail on the other side of the fire road. The trail immediately climbs a few yards and drops briefly before beginning a long, continuous ascent back to the west parking lot. Because this trail section parallels the paved road, you will catch glimpses of it here and there as you climb through the pine forest.

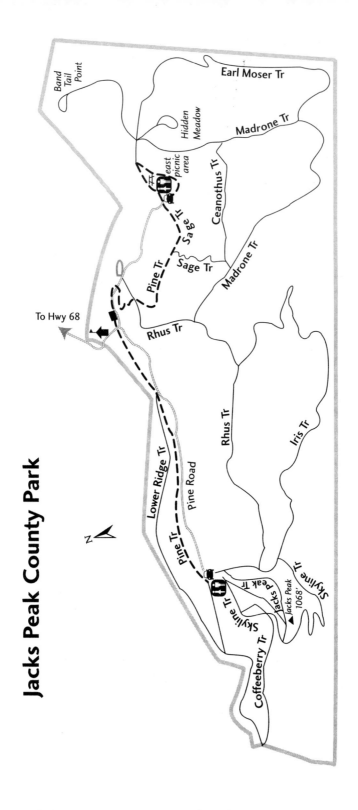

Jacks Peak County Park

Band Tail Point

Earl Moser Tr

Hidden Meadow

Madrone Tr

east picnic area

Ceanothus Tr

Sage Tr

Sage Tr

Pine Tr

Madrone Tr

To Hwy 68

Rhus Tr

Rhus Tr

Iris Tr

Lower Ridge Tr

Pine Road

Pine Tr

N

Skyline Tr

Jacks Peak Tr

Jacks Peak 1068'

Skyline Tr

Coffeeberry Tr

West Lot to East Lot Loop

Distance: 4 miles   Difficulty: 👟👟

This end-to-end loop run is my favorite. When I want a good work-out at Jacks Peak that provides variation in terrain, atmosphere and scenery, but I don't have time or energy to do the longer runs described in this guide, this is the route I choose.

While the run can begin from either parking lot, I describe it from the west lot to the east lot and back, closing the loop.

Having reached the west parking lot by turning right and driving from the entrance kiosk, you find a steel-pole gate and a pay phone to the right just as you enter the lot. Your trail for this route begins behind and to the right of the pay phone. The initial trail, mostly a gentle downhill, parallels the paved road all the way back to the kiosk. About a quarter mile before reaching the kiosk, you pass another steel-pole gate just off the paved road that blocks entry to a fire road coming in from your left. Keep straight ahead, parallel to the gate and paved road. Immediately the trail climbs steeply for 100 yards and then levels off for another 100 before dropping quickly to the kiosk.

Cross the paved road and pass the kiosk on its downhill side in order to pick up the trail. This section climbs briefly up to the paved entrance to the park's maintenance yard. Cross the pavement to pick up the trail opposite, which winds for 100 yards before turning abruptly right toward the paved road. Cross the road at this point to pick up the obvious trail on the other side.

27

This trail section descends quickly down a set of switchbacks until reaching a junction with a fire road. Cross the fire road to pick up the *Pine Trail* on the other side. The next section begins an immediate climb up and toward the right, winding around a hillside. After 100 yards it levels off and drops into a ravine before starting another steep climb to another trail junction.

At the next junction turn left onto an open hillside, which provides enticing views of Carmel Valley and the mountains beyond. Because this unshaded section is very rocky and steep, on a sunny day you will feel the heat. After climbing up to a hump the trail drops briefly, giving your legs a break before you begin a gentle climb to the east parking lot.

As soon as you hit the parking-lot pavement, swing right toward the bathroom building. To the right a fire road circles behind the building and the BBQ/picnic area on a rise. Stay on this fire road circling the *East Picnic Area* until you reach the top of a steep, short climb, bringing you to a junction with another fire road. Turn left and drop down behind the other BBQ area. You will be on a short section of the *Earl Moser Trail* until you return to the pavement in about a 100 yards.

Now cross the parking lot to near where the road enters, and retrace your route on the same trail you came in on for the return leg. Pay attention so you don't take any wrong turns, or you will end up running many more and harder miles—to the "outback" of Jacks Peak Park!

Jacks Peak with a view of Carmel Valley and the Ventana Wilderness

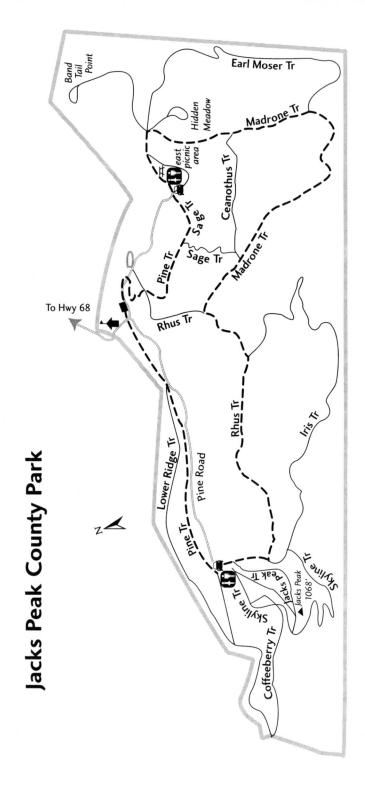

Jacks Peak County Park

Band Tail Point

Earl Moser Tr

Hidden Meadow

Madrone Tr

east picnic area

Ceanothus Tr

Sage Tr

Sage Tr

Pine Tr

Madrone Tr

Rhus Tr

To Hwy 68

Rhus Tr

Iris Tr

Lower Ridge Tr

Pine Road

Pine Tr

N

Skyline Tr

Jacks Peak Tr

Jacks Peak 1068'

Skyline Tr

Coffeeberry Tr

Run **5**

Great Inner Loop

Distance: 5 miles   Difficulty: 👟👟👟

This is one loop that will challenge you no matter which direction you
run it: uphills in one direction are no easier than those in the other.
But one very long uphill will test you more than any other at Jacks
Peak Park.

Turn right at the entrance kiosk and drive to the west parking lot.
Find a steel-pole gate and a pay phone to the right just as you enter
the lot. Your trail for this route begins behind and to the right of the
pay phone. The initial trail, mostly a gentle downhill, parallels the
paved road all the way back to the kiosk. About a quarter mile before
reaching the kiosk, you pass another steel-pole gate just off the paved
road that blocks entry to a fire road coming in from your left. Keep
straight ahead, parallel to the gate and paved road. Immediately the
trail climbs steeply for 100 yards and then levels off for another 100
before dropping quickly to the kiosk.

Cross the paved road and pass the kiosk on its downhill side in
order to pick up the trail. This section climbs briefly up to the paved
entrance to the park's maintenance yard. Cross the pavement to pick
up the trail opposite, which winds for 100 yards before turning
abruptly right toward the paved road. Cross the road at this point to
pick up the obvious trail on the other side.

This trail section descends quickly down a set of switchbacks
until reaching a junction with a fire road. Cross the fire road to pick
up another trail on the other side. The next section begins an imme-

31

diate climb up and toward the right, winding around a hillside. After 100 yards it levels off and drops into a ravine before starting another steep climb to another trail junction.

At the next junction turn left onto an open hillside, which provides enticing views of Carmel Valley and the mountains beyond. Because this unshaded section is very rocky and steep, on a sunny day you will feel the heat. After climbing up to a hump the trail drops briefly, giving your legs a break before you begin a gentle climb to the east parking lot.

South of the lot is a bathroom building. While the loop could begin at three different points, if you look north of the lot, away from the bathroom, you will see a sign designating the start of the *Earl Moser Trail*.

For 100 yards the trail dips past the BBQ/picnic area, then it climbs briefly to a junction. Continuing straight ahead you soon drop steeply down to a five-way junction. Take the hard right turn onto the fire road, which descends steeply for about 100 yards. On the park map this section is called the *Madrone Trail*. This fire road will be your trail for the next few miles. Most of the trails in the core of Jacks Peak Park are really fire roads, but the park calls them trails and that is how they are used.

Once this trail levels off you cruise for over a half mile along a gentle downhill slope. You pass the *Ceanothus Trail* coming in from the right. Continue straight ahead. When you reach another junction, where *Run 2* makes its return, pass it and keep right as the trail curves. Over the next quarter mile you climb briefly, coming out into a more open area before beginning a long and steep descent. For the next mile you descend, then level off, with only one short, steep climb. At the top of this rise note a yellow fire hydrant on your left. There are a few along this route and one marks a "key" junction for this route (as does one for *Run 6*).

Just past this rise is another junction with the *Ceanothus Trail* on the right. Again, pass it. Leaving the *Madrone Trail* at the next T-junction, bear left onto the *Rhus Trail* (you pass a hydrant here on the right). You now run a short distance on the level, curving through shady overhead brush. Approaching the next "key" junction, you will see another yellow hydrant straight ahead and up a short slope to the left. Here the *Iris Trail* splits left from the *Rhus Trail*. You continue ahead, passing the hydrant on your left, to remain on the *Rhus Trail*.

Beyond this junction you reach the longest and most difficult uphill in Jacks Peak Park. You must ascend relentlessly up a very steep incline for nearly a mile. You may find it necessary to "down-shift" in order to complete this long uphill without stopping.

This gruelling uphill ends at a welcome, flat trail junction. Turn right here and climb gently the short distance back to the west parking lot.

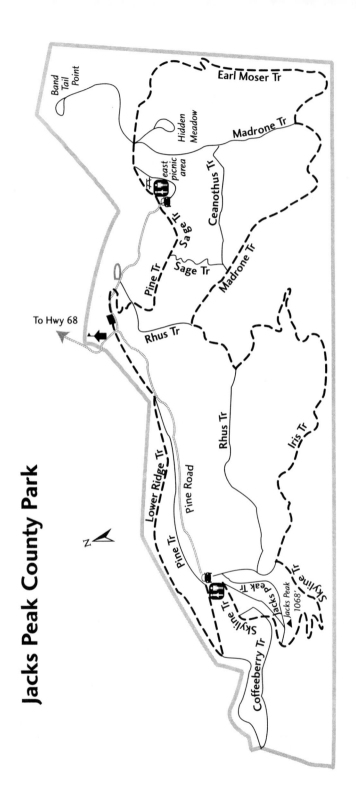

Jacks Peak County Park

Band Tail Point

Earl Moser Tr

Hidden Meadow

Madrone Tr

east picnic area

Ceanothus Tr

Sage Tr

Sage Tr

Madrone Tr

Pine Tr

To Hwy 68

Rhus Tr

Rhus Tr

Iris Tr

Lower Ridge Tr

Pine Road

Pine Tr

N

Jacks Peak Tr

Jacks Peak 1068'

Skyline Tr

Skyline Tr

Coffeeberry Tr

Run **6**

Great Outer Loop

Distance: 7 miles   Difficulty: 👟👟👟

This grand tour of Jacks Peak Park comprises all the other routes and then some. When you've completed this run you will know you've had a workout, but beyond the calories burned and the sweat pumped, you will be treated to the full range of aesthetic variety that Jacks Peak Park has to offer.

Start this route at the west parking lot; turn right at the entrance kiosk and drive to the road's end. Find the start of this route just behind the bathroom building.

For the first quarter mile you drop rapidly down a steep fire road to a junction with another fire road. Turn right and cruise for just over another quarter mile along a gentle downgrade. Shortly after this road levels off, it begins a long, gentle upward climb to a steel-pole gate where the fire road merges with the paved main road (heading to the west parking lot). The trail continues just to the left of the gate. The trail now climbs steeply for about 100 yards and then levels off for another 100. After that it drops quickly down to the entrance kiosk.

Cross the paved road and pass the kiosk on its downhill side in order to pick up the trail. This section climbs briefly up to the paved entrance to the park's maintenance yard. Cross the pavement to pick up the trail opposite, which winds for 100 yards before turning abruptly right toward the paved road. Cross the road at this point to pick up the obvious trail on the other side.

35

This trail section descends quickly down a set of switchbacks until reaching a junction with a fire road. Cross the fire road to pick up *Pine Trail* on the other side. The next section begins an immediate climb up and toward the right, winding around a hillside. After 100 yards the trail levels off, then drops into a ravine, before starting another steep climb to another trail junction.

At the next junction turn left onto an open hillside, which provides enticing views of Carmel Valley and the mountains beyond. Because this unshaded section is very rocky and steep, on a sunny day you will feel the heat. After climbing up to a hump the trail drops briefly, giving your legs a break before you begin a gentle climb to the east parking lot.

South of the lot is a bathroom building. If you look north of the lot, away from the bathroom, you will see a sign designating the start of the *Earl Moser Trail*. For 100 yards the trail dips past the BBQ/picnic area, then it climbs briefly to a junction. Continuing straight ahead you soon drop steeply down a fire road to a five-way junction. Straight ahead a wooden sign confirms you're on the *Earl Moser Trail*.

The trail now begins a long steep climb with a switchback here and there—a calf-burner! Almost relentlessly uphill for a good half mile, the trail has only a few, brief level and downhill stretches to allow you some recovery. But the "burn" is worth the effort, because once the trail levels off you are treated to a long cruise through pines and meadows, across a mesa-like ridgetop.

Along this ridgetop you pass a bench on the right side of the trail. Not far beyond it the trail begins its descent. Left of the trail you see a barbed-wire fence that marks the boundary between public and private lands. The trail soon comes to a steep downhill set of steps with a railing. At the bottom of these steps a road descends steeply to a junction with the *Madrone Trail*. Turn Left.

Over the next quarter mile you climb briefly, coming out into a more open area before beginning a long and steep descent. For the next mile you descend, then level off, with only one short, steep climb. At the top of this rise note a yellow fire hydrant on your left. There are a few along this route and one marks a "key" junction for this route.

Just past this rise is a junction with the *Ceanothus Trail* on the right. Pass it. Leaving the *Madrone Trail* at the next T-junction, bear left onto the *Rhus Trail* (you pass a hydrant here on the right). You now run a short distance on the level, curving through shady overhead brush. Approaching the next "key" junction, you will see another yellow hydrant straight ahead and up a short slope to the left. Here the *Rhus Trail* continues ahead. You split left onto the *Iris Trail*, passing the hydrant on your right.

The trail drops gently for about 50 yards. It then begins a long arduous climb. For the next mile you get three major climbs with only brief level and downhill sections in between to give your legs short reprieves. After the third climb, the trail descends for about a quarter mile, giving you time to recover before the next two.

The first of these next two climbs is the longest. It tops out with a nice level section followed by a short and steep downhill. At the bottom of this downhill you immediately begin another long, steep climb.

After about a quarter mile you will see where *Run 1* (*Skyline Trail*) comes in from the left. Turn left at this junction and follow *Run 1's* route description in reverse to return to the west parking lot. By doing so, you get to top off this grand tour by running uphill on the switchbacks. Feel the burn!

"

Run for fun, not competition.

It's enough to run against gravity

and time. **"**

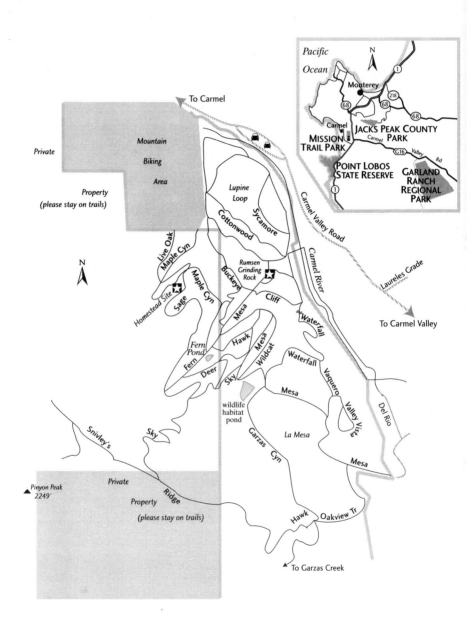

Garland Ranch Regional Park

Garland Ranch Regional Park

ALL BUT ONE TRAIL OF GARLAND RANCH PARK, ALONG THE BANKS OF THE CARMEL RIVER IN THE HEART OF THAT VALLEY, WIND UP the steep north-facing slope of the ridge south of the valley. I've chosen only two runs to feature in this park: the first an easy one over mostly flat terrain, the other a very long, gruelling climb to the top of the ridge.

During the rainy season, sections of the upper trails get muddy and slippery. In late spring, summer, and early fall, Carmel Valley can get quite hot, often with temperatures greater than 100°F. Because running at Garland Ranch during the hot months is a challenge greater than I desire, I run here during cooler and drier times of the year.

As at Jacks Peak Park, cougars have been sighted here. With your solitude on the upper trails assured, be alert to the same safety factors mentioned for Jacks Peak Park.

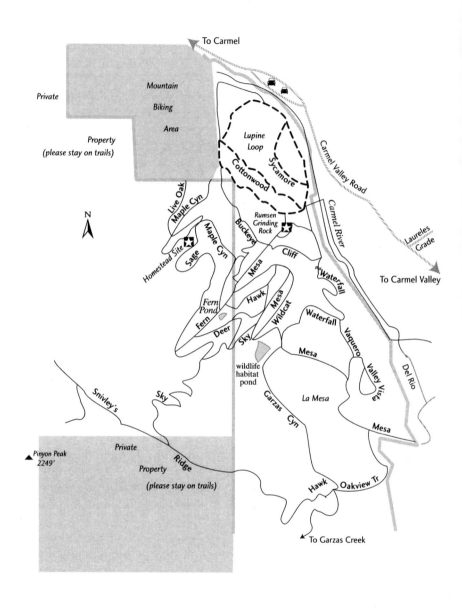

To Carmel

Private

Mountain

Biking

Area

Property
(please stay on trails)

Lupine
Loop

Cottonwood

Sycamore

Carmel Valley Road

Live Oak

Maple Cyn

Buckeye

Rumsen
Grinding
Rock

Carmel River

Laureles
Grade

N

Maple Cyn

Mesa

Cliff

To Carmel Valley

Homestead Site

Sage

Waterfall

Fern
Pond

Hawk

Mesa

Fern

Deer

Sky

Wildcat

Waterfall

Waterfall

Vaquero

Valley Vista

Del Rio

Mesa

Sky

wildlife
habitat
pond

Mesa

La Mesa

Mesa

Snivley's

Sky

Pinyon Peak
2249'

Private

Ridge

Garzas Cyn

Property

(please stay on trails)

Hawk

Oakview Tr

To Garzas Creek

Garland Ranch Regional Park

River Floodplain Loop

Distance: 2+ miles   Difficulty: 👟

This Garland Ranch run is the easiest one in the guidebook. Other than one brief and gentle uphill, this flat route zigzags across the gravelly floodplain created over thousands of years by the seasonal flow of the Carmel River.

The route begins and ends at the *Visitor Center* located in an upriver clearing, which you see left of the steel automobile bridge spanning the river before you enter the dirt parking area. There's also a wooden footbridge that crosses the river on the other side of the *Visitor Center*, but this bridge is impassable during the high water of heavy winter storms.

With your back to the *Visitor Center* and the river, you face south. Start this route by taking the trail that heads west—back toward the steel bridge and parallel to the river. When you get almost to the dirt road that goes over the bridge, turn left and follow the trail south along a fenceline. A "straight shot" for a few hundred yards, the trail now climbs ever so gently toward the hills. Soon the trail curves left (away from the *Buckeye Trail*) and continues a slightly steeper climb beneath oak trees that skirt the floodplain. For a few hundred yards you cruise along this gently rolling section, passing a couple of benches, until you come to the junction with the *Mesa Trail*. As you curve left and downward, away from the *Mesa Trail*, you pass another nearby bench.

41

Carmel River crossing at Garland Ranch

Now, heading back down onto the floodplain, you quickly encounter a junction to your left for the *Cottonwood Trail*, one of two short trails that cross the floodplain. Pass this junction and continue a short distance to the next. Turn left onto the *Sycamore Trail*. It bows west before eventually rejoining the main trail.

At the next junction with the main trail, turn right and head south—back in the direction from which you started. Keep on this trail, passing the *Sycamore Trail* again to your right, until you retrace your steps to the *Cottonwood Trail* junction again. Now turn right and follow the *Cottonwood Trail* until it rejoins the main trail along the earlier encountered fenceline. Turn right and head back toward the steel bridge. Just before the bridge, a right turn will take you back to the *Visitor Center*.

"

Run within your breath. Fatigue and demoralization set in when you push beyond your body's ability to provide the oxygen necessary to keep your muscles from tiring. "

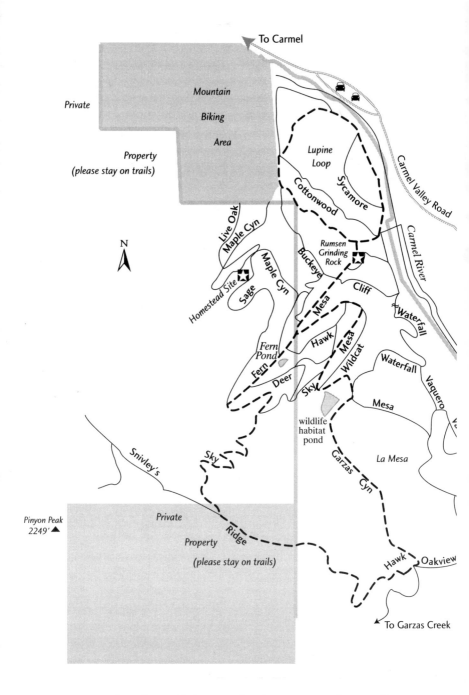

Garland Ranch Regional Park

Run 8

Upper Mesa Loop

Distance: 6+ miles   Difficulty: 👟👟👟👟

I include this route for the uphill fanatics! Over the past decade I've done this run a dozen or so times when I wanted to gauge my level of fitness. The more times I have to stop and shake out my cramping legs the less fit I am, or so I assume. I can recall one time that I did this entire route without stopping; it was 20 years ago.

This run begins by following part of the route from the last one. With your back to the *Visitor Center* and the river, face south. Take the trail that heads north—back toward the steel bridge and parallel to the river. When you get almost to the dirt road that goes over the bridge, turn left and follow the trail south along a fenceline. A "straight shot" for a few hundred yards, the trail now climbs ever so gently toward the hills. Soon the trail curves left (away from the *Buckeye Trail*) and continues a slightly steeper climb beneath oak trees that skirt the floodplain. For a few hundred yards you cruise along this gently rolling section, passing a couple of benches, until you come to the junction with the *Mesa Trail*.

Turn right on the *Mesa Trail* and begin a very long and gruelling climb toward the summit of Snivley's Ridge. About a half mile uphill you come to a junction where the *Mesa Trail* goes left, the *Fern Trail* continues straight ahead, and the *Maple Canyon Trail* comes in from the right. Continue climbing straight ahead on the *Fern Trail*. In another half mile you reach a junction where the *Sage Trail* comes in from the right. Turn left here. The trail levels a bit as it curves around

45

_ı canyon. Soon you come to the junction with the *Sky Trail*.
_nt and continue up a gruelling set of switchbacks toward the
_etop.

After a half mile you reach the top and a T-junction with *Snivley's Ridge Trail*. To your right the trail makes a very long descent to Carmel Valley. A spur trail in that direction leads to an abandoned fire lookout visible from here. To your immediate left are the remains of an old corral. Take this left and pass the corral to begin an extremely steep drop down Snivley's Ridge.

You descend for almost a mile to a junction with the *Garzas Canyon Trail*. Turn left and continue your quick descent until the trail begins to level off on the mesa, where you'll see a large pond ahead on your left. Shortly after the pond you reach a junction with the *Waterfall Trail*. Bear left here on the *Mesa Trail*. You lose more elevation as the trail curves left around a hillside before climbing to an earlier junction with the *Fern Trail*. Take a sharp right to retrace your steps steeply downhill on the *Mesa Trail*.

Once again you pick up the route described in the last run. At the next junction turn right and quickly descend onto the floodplain, passing a nearby bench. You quickly encounter a junction left for the *Cottonwood Trail*. Pass it and continue a short distance to the next. Turn left onto the *Sycamore Trail*. It bows west before eventually rejoining the main trail.

River flood Plain Loop

At the next junction with the main trail, turn right and head south—back in the direction from which you started. Keep on this trail, passing the *Sycamore Trail* again to your right, until you retrace your steps to the *Cottonwood Trail* junction again. Now turn right and follow the *Cottonwood Trail* until it rejoins the main trail along the earlier encountered fenceline. Turn right and head back toward the steel bridge. Just before the bridge, a right turn will take you back to the *Visitor Center.*

> **If you need to stop during a run, do it! With nothing to prove to anyone—not even yourself—don't push beyond your reasonable limits. A brief rest can recharge your batteries and makes the run more enjoyable.**

To Carmel
4 miles

Ichxenta Point

Reserve Boundary

EXTREMELY
DANGEROUS
SURF ZONE

Moss Cove Tr

Escobar Rocks

Moss Cove

Hudson
House

Kodani
Village

*Granite
Point*

Granite Point Tr

Carmelo Meadow Tr

The
Pit

Coal
Chute Point

Whalers Cove

*Carmelo
Meadow*

Pacific

Cannery
Point

Mound
Meadow Tr

Whalers Cabin
(museum)

North Shore Tr

Cabin Tr

Ocean

*Bluefish
Cove*

Lace Lichen Tr

Pine Ridge Tr

Guillemot Island

*East
Grove*

Whalers Knoll Tr

Piney
Woods

*Terminal
Rock*

Whalers
Knoll

*Big
Dome*

Old Veteran Tr

Sand Hill Tr

Cypress Cove

Old Veteran

Sea Lion Point Tr

Sand Hill Cove

Cypress Grove Tr

*North
Point*

Allan
Memorial
Grove

Sea Lion Cove

*South
Point*

Headland
Cove

*Punta De Los
Lobos Marinos*

*Devil's
Cauldron*

The Pinnacle

*Pinnacle
Cove*

*Sea
Lion
Rocks*

N

Point Lobos State Reserve

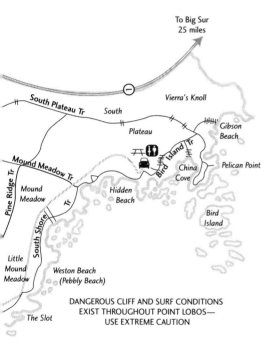

To Big Sur
25 miles

South Plateau Tr

Vierra's Knoll

South
Plateau

Gibson
Beach

Mound Meadow Tr

Bird Island Tr

China
Cove

Pelican Point

Pine Ridge Tr

Mound
Meadow

Hidden
Beach

Bird
Island

South Shore Tr

Little
Mound
Meadow

Weston Beach
(Pebbly Beach)

DANGEROUS CLIFF AND SURF CONDITIONS
EXIST THROUGHOUT POINT LOBOS—
USE EXTREME CAUTION

The Slot

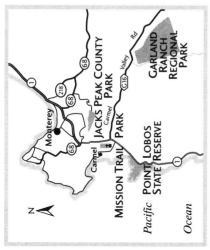

JACKS PEAK COUNTY PARK

GARLAND RANCH REGIONAL PARK

Carmel Valley Rd

G16

Monterey

MISSION TRAIL PARK

Carmel

POINT LOBOS STATE RESERVE

Pacific

Ocean

N

Point Lobos State Reserve

THE JEWEL OF THE MONTEREY COUNTY PARKS SYSTEM ADORNING THE OCEAN'S SHORE, POINT LOBOS STATE RESERVE IS A SPECtacularly situated trail runner's paradise with a fantastic selection of routes through a pine forest. A wide variety of distances and difficulties allow you to get whatever level of workout you desire while exhilarating every sense. With scenery second to none, Point Lobos is a must for any trail runner.

Point Lobos was the first trail venue I ran—on moving to the Monterey Peninsula almost 30 years ago—and I've had a love affair with it ever since. Yet, due to the explosion of tourist traffic on the highway and the increased pedestrian traffic within the reserve in the last decade, it has sometimes felt like a love/hate relationship. I once felt as though Point Lobos belonged to me because I could run there anytime of the day or week in solitude; now I run there on weekdays when it first opens or just before closing. Forget holidays or weekends! Perhaps due to the opening of the Monterey Bay Aquarium in the mid-

1980s, the world has discovered the Monterey Peninsula: unlimited and uncrowded access is history.

Though a must for any trail runner, choose the times you visit Point Lobos very carefully to avoid having to yell "Excuse me!" every few yards on the trail, and the hour-long traffic backup returning to peninsula cities.

The Pine Ridge Trail at Point Lobos with a view across Mound Meadow to the ocean

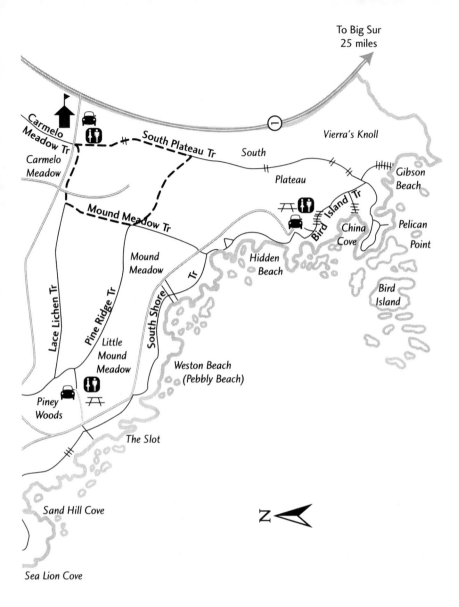

To Big Sur
25 miles

Carmelo Meadow Tr

South Plateau Tr

Vierra's Knoll

Carmelo Meadow

South

Plateau

Gibson Beach

Mound Meadow Tr

Bird Island Tr

China Cove

Pelican Point

Mound Meadow

Hidden Beach

Bird Island

Lace Lichen Tr

Pine Ridge Tr

South Shore Tr

Little Mound Meadow

Weston Beach (Pebbly Beach)

Piney Woods

The Slot

Sand Hill Cove

N

Sea Lion Cove

DANGEROUS CLIFF AND SURF CONDITIONS
EXIST THROUGHOUT POINT LOBOS—
USE EXTREME CAUTION

Sea Lion Rocks

Point Lobos State Reserve

South 1-Mile Loop

Distance: 1 mile   Difficulty: 👟

This is a great little loop for those who are not yet fit for the harder routes or who only have time for a quick run. It gives you a taste of Point Lobos.

Just beyond the entrance kiosk you will see your trailhead to the left (south). For the first 100 yards on the *South Plateau Trail* you run levelly or on a slight upgrade. Next, the trail winds and climbs moderately steeply for another 100 yards, before beginning a long, windy downhill. Be careful not to trip over the network of tree roots that protrude above the ground. I once caught my toe on one of these roots and took a horrendous spill. Be alert while running on the trails at Point Lobos, and pick up your feet as you negotiate the roots and rocks.

Where the trail levels off, you reach a junction with the *Pine Ridge Trail*. Turn right. You descend gradually for 100 yards and then level off for an easy cruise through the forest. At the next junction—with the *Mound Meadow Trail*—turn right and begin an immediate uphill climb for a 100 yards. Following this short climb you level off for the rest of the run. The route now winds through woods until reaching the paved entrance road. Turn right and run along the dirt shoulder back to the kiosk.

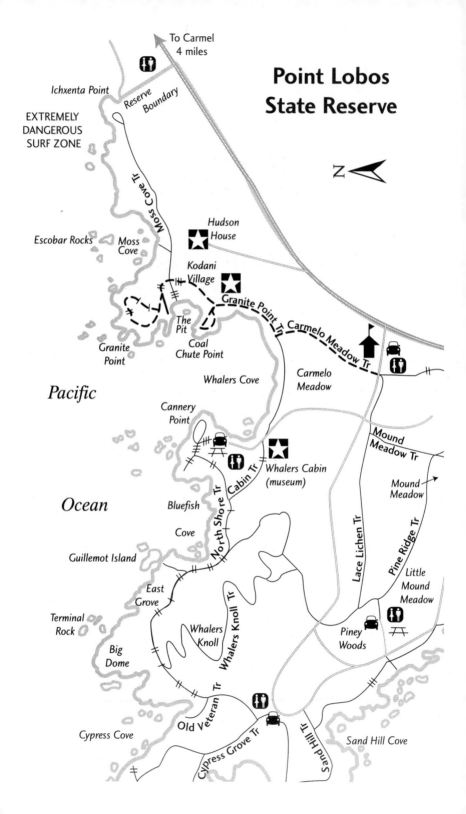

North 2-Mile Loop

Distance: 2+ miles   Difficulty: 👟

This terrific little run gives you a good workout amid spectacular scenery. It's not unusual to see sea birds, herons, sea lions, harbor seals, and other wildlife along this cliffside route.

Just past the entrance kiosk you will see your trailhead on the right. The first several yards are flat, but then you take an abrupt right to begin a gradual descent for a few hundred yards through a forested area. This trail section used to be called the *Carmelo Meadow Trail* but was recently rerouted away from the meadow and has not yet been renamed. Where the trail abruptly opens out into a view of *Whalers Cove*, you immediately reach a T-junction with the *Granite Point Trail* and turn right.

The *Granite Point Trail* winds in and out of the woods offering occasional views of *Whalers Cove*. You run along a cliff at one point where you can look down to its crescent-shaped, dark sand beach. Then you drop into a section of trail pleasingly canopied with flowering shrubs. Slow down here because just beyond is a trail junction to your left. Turn left to circle *Coal Chute Point*, which affords fantastic views of coast wildlife. Circle this point in either direction; either way you get some short but steep, uphill switchbacks.

After completing this circle you continue left on the *Granite Point Trail*. Your route is relatively flat for the next 200 yards, but then you descend a flight of crude steps to a junction. A right turn here would take you out across a wide-open area to the northern boundary of Point Lobos. A sharp left turn would take you down to a rocky beach known as *The Pit*. But another set of crude steps lies directly opposite. Take them to begin a curving climb up to *Granite Point*.

There are some potential false turns along this section, where there appear to be trail junctions, but the attentive runner will easily find the main trail. After 100 uphill yards through brush cover, you come to a junction. Make a loop of *Granite Point* in either direction. Be careful: there are plenty of places to trip over protruding rocks and take a nasty spill. You circle this point around and beneath a prominent granite monolith at its center. After completing this loop head back to the kiosk the way you came, once again circling *Coal Chute Point*, perhaps now in the other direction.

Coal Chute Point

Ancient Indian grinding pits at the north park boundary of Point Lobos Reserve

"

Running with a partner of equal ability eases the most difficult run. If you calibrate your pace with conversation, the miles pass without drudgery.   *"*

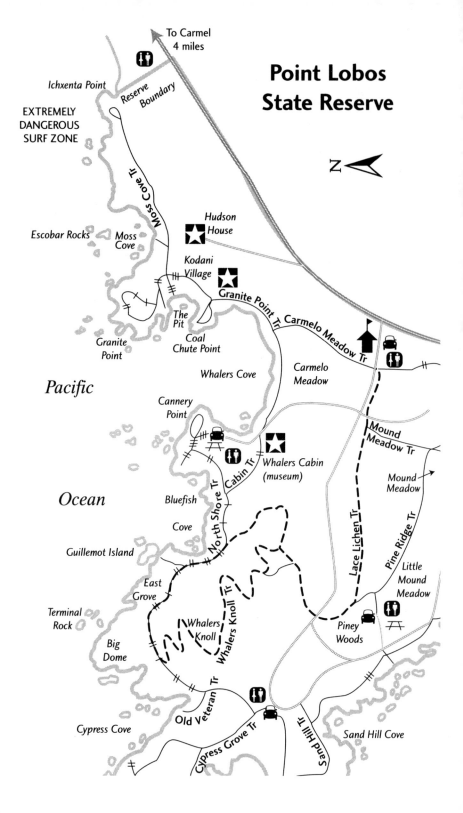

Whalers Knoll Loop

Distance: 3+ miles   Difficulty: 👟👟👟

If you want a demanding workout without having to run a long distance, this is it! From the top of *Whalers Knoll* the scenery is simply spectacular. Remarkably, this highest trail point within Point Lobos is rarely visited by the typical tourist.

From the entrance kiosk run west along the left side of the paved road, preferably on the dirt shoulder. At the first junction with a service road, angle off left toward an obvious intersection with the *Lace Lichen Trail*. Although the *Mound Meadow Trail* also comes in here from the left, take the *Lace Lichen Trail* west, parallel to the main paved road. The road remains within sight and sound for several hundred yards.

After about a half mile you reach a junction with the *Pine Ridge Trail* entering from the left. Continue straight ahead. Shortly past this junction the trail curves right, back toward the paved road. Cross the road to pick up the trail on the other side.

Across the road the trail curves right and parallels it for a short distance before swinging back left to begin a long, arduous climb toward *Whalers Knoll*. You climb several hundred yards until you reach what has the appearance of a pass, marked by a weathered, round metal plate on the ground to your right here (the cover for an abandoned shut-off valve).

At this pass is a key junction. Either take an immediate left and continue an even steeper climb up switchbacks toward the summit of

Summit Bench at Whalers Knoll

Whalers Knoll, or drop down the other side of the pass to reach another junction a few yards downhill. This second option adds distance and variety to your ascent.

At this second junction just below the pass, turn left and begin a long, steep climb up along the northeast side of *Whalers Knoll*. If you dare to take your eyes off the tricky trail underfoot, look down the hillside for views of beautiful coves far below. Monarch butterflies roost in the pines in winter along this uphill stretch.

The trail turns sharply left along a switchback, and then curves right to pass under a large, leaning pine. Just past this tree is the junction where the first option from the pass (left) joins your route to the top of *Whalers Knoll*. Bearing right where the trail snakes its way around some thick pine trees will let you climb at an easier incline. The uphill stretch soon ends and you begin a gentle descent to the highlight of this route.

Emerging from the trees you'll come upon a bench with WHALERS KNOLL carved into it. So beautiful is this spot and the view that my wife and I chose to be married here in 1985. As you run through this summit area constituting the knoll, watch your footing because the trail is quarried right out of a granite shelf. For several yards down from the summit, twisting an ankle or falling are real possibilities to be avoided.

Below this rocky area the trail descends via switchbacks to a junction with the *North Shore Trail*. Turn right. You now roller-coaster beneath the looming presence of *Whalers Knoll* to your right. After 200 yards you reach the top of a long set of crude steps that curve to the left. At the bottom is a treacherous rocky area that you must cross to reach the trail continuation beyond it. A wrong step here could mean a very bad fall.

Once past this rocky ledge, go a short distance to a junction under the outstretched limbs of cypress trees. Turn right and immediately begin climbing granite steps. For the next 200 yards the trail undulates radically over rocks, roots, and steps—obstacles and potential pitfalls for the inattentive. The views, if you dare to deflect attention from the rugged trail, are fantastic through this section.

Just past a set of steep crude steps that descend to the left, you climb briefly to a junction (left is the root mass of a large overturned pine). Turn right and begin a long, steep climb back up the northeast side of *Whalers Knoll* toward the aforementioned pass. If you don't want to end up climbing the knoll again, when you come to the next critical junction, turn left and head briefly back up to the pass. You'll know you've arrived when you look down to your left and see that metal plate in the ground. From the pass you return to the kiosk the way you came.

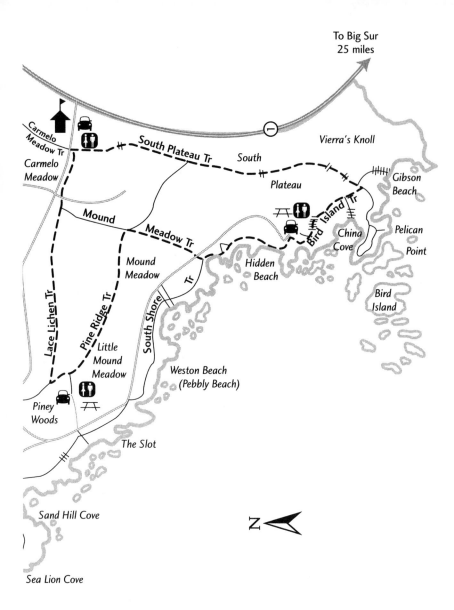

To Big Sur
25 miles

Carmelo
Meadow Tr

Carmelo
Meadow

South Plateau Tr

South

Plateau

Vierra's Knoll

Gibson
Beach

Mound

Meadow Tr

Bird Island Tr

China
Cove

Pelican
Point

Mound
Meadow

Hidden
Beach

Bird
Island

Lace Lichen Tr

Pine Ridge Tr

South Shore

Tr

Little
Mound
Meadow

Weston Beach
(Pebbly Beach)

Piney
Woods

The Slot

Sand Hill Cove

N

Sea Lion Cove

DANGEROUS CLIFF AND SURF CONDITIONS
EXIST THROUGHOUT POINT LOBOS—
USE EXTREME CAUTION

Sea
Lion
Rocks

Point Lobos State Reserve

South Inner Forest Loop

Distance: 3 miles   **Difficulty:** 👟👟

This medium-length run gives you a full sampling of what Point Lobos has to offer: forest and rugged coast. It's a good workout without the gruelling hills of the other longer runs here.

Just beyond the entrance kiosk you will see your trailhead to the left (south). For the first 100 yards on the *South Plateau Trail* you run levelly or on a slight upgrade. Next, the trail winds and climbs moderately steeply for another 100 yards, before beginning a long, windy downhill. Be careful not to trip over the network of tree roots that protrude above the ground. Where the trail levels off, you reach a junction with the *Pine Ridge Trail*.

You continue straight ahead, cross a short split-log footbridge, and begin a short, steep climb over a small rise. Your downhill stretch is longer than the ascent in this direction. Below the rise the trail levels off and winds through pines for 100 yards. Then, after a long moderate climb topping out at a large pine (left), the trail descends a brushy south-facing slope. Descending a first set of crude steps and zigzagging left and right down more, you'll see Point Lobos' southernmost *Gibson Beach*, which marks the southern boundary. Stay on the trail curving (right) through the brush and you will come to the junction with the *Bird Island Trail*. Turn right and make your way along a cliff overlooking the emerald-green water of *China Cove*.

Bird Island Trail descends a long set of crude steps to the reserve's south parking lot. Skirt the left side of the lot, heading slightly downhill, to pick up the trail near where the road enters. Wind your way along the *South Shore Trail*, which hugs the shoreline to your left. It zigzags through brush for a few hundred yards. Keep the paved road to your right and avoid any spur trails that lead to the rocky beaches. A section of the trail makes a prominent horseshoe bend around a small rocky cove. Beyond this bend you come to a sandstone conglomerate shelf that creates a significant hump in the trail. Run up and over it, watching your footing. Just past this hump is the junction with the *Mound Meadow Trail*, where you turn right and cross the paved road.

The next 200 yards are flat and straight, as the trail heads through tree cover with a large meadow on the left. At the next trail junction turn left on the *Pine Ridge Trail* and begin a gradual climb west through brush. The trail climbs gently for 100 yards and then levels off for several hundred more. It curves around a mound that overlooks most of the reserve's southwest shoreline.

Beyond a bench the trail curves right; then a spur trail comes in from the left. If you turned left here you'd drop right down to a parking lot and picnic area. Instead, head right and continue winding through high brush. Where the trail opens into a clearing, you reach a junction with the *Lace Lichen Trail*. Turn right and parallel the main road back to the entrance kiosk.

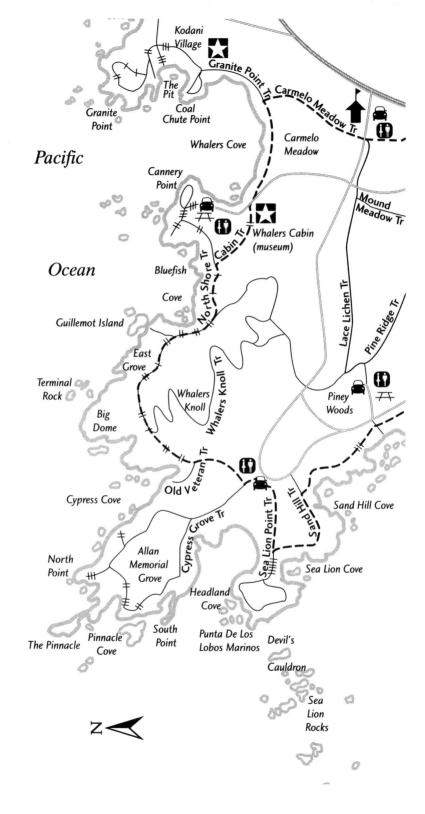

Pacific

Ocean

Kodani Village

Granite Point Tr

Carmelo Meadow Tr

The Pit

Coal Chute Point

Granite Point

Whalers Cove

Carmelo Meadow

Mound Meadow Tr

Cannery Point

Whalers Cabin (museum)

Cabin Tr

North Shore Tr

Lace Lichen Tr

Pine Ridge Tr

Bluefish Cove

Guillemot Island

East Grove

Whalers Knoll Tr

Whalers Knoll

Piney Woods

Terminal Rock

Big Dome

Old Veteran Tr

Cypress Cove

Cypress Grove Tr

Sea Lion Point Tr

Sand Hill Tr

Sand Hill Cove

North Point

Allan Memorial Grove

Sea Lion Cove

Headland Cove

The Pinnacle

Pinnacle Cove

South Point

Punta De Los Lobos Marinos

Devil's Cauldron

Sea Lion Rocks

N

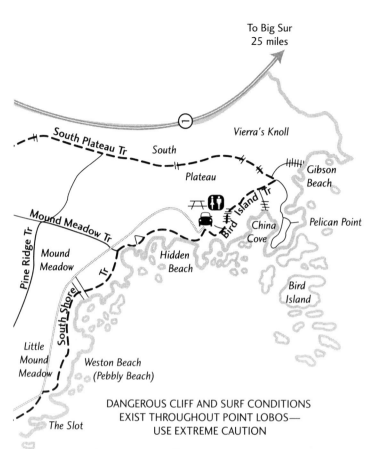

To Big Sur
25 miles

Vierra's Knoll

South Plateau Tr

South
Plateau

Gibson
Beach

Bird Island Tr

China
Cove

Pelican Point

Mound Meadow Tr

Pine Ridge Tr

Mound
Meadow

Hidden
Beach

Bird
Island

South Shore Tr

Little
Mound
Meadow

Weston Beach
(Pebbly Beach)

DANGEROUS CLIFF AND SURF CONDITIONS
EXIST THROUGHOUT POINT LOBOS—
USE EXTREME CAUTION

The Slot

Point Lobos State Reserve

Run 13

Outer 3.5–Mile Loop

Outer 3.5–Mile Loop

Distance: 3.5 miles   Difficulty: 👟👟

This classic Point Lobos loop gives you many short but hard hills, plenty of flats to kick out any tightness after the hills, and thrilling scenery to take your mind off the effort. Because of its popularity with tourists, I suggest you run this route when Point Lobos first opens in the morning or about an hour before it closes in the late afternoon.

I used to do four consecutive laps at a single time on this loop, and in 1976 I established my personal record of 21:29 for a single lap. That's a 6-minute-mile pace, a rather fast time for such a rugged trail route. Today I'm content to run this loop in a comfortable 30 minutes.

Just beyond the entrance kiosk you will see your trailhead to the left (south). For the first 100 yards on the *South Plateau Trail* you run levelly or on a slight upgrade. Next the trail winds and climbs moderately steeply for another 100 yards, before beginning a long, windy downhill. Be careful not trip over the network of tree roots that protrude above the ground. Where the trail levels off, you reach a junction with the *Pine Ridge Trail*.

You continue straight ahead, cross a short split-log footbridge, and begin a short, steep climb over a small rise. Your downhill stretch is longer than the ascent in this direction. Below the rise the trail levels off and winds through pines for 100 yards. Then, after a long moderate climb topping out at a large pine (left), the trail descends a brushy south-facing slope. Descending a first set of crude steps and

Carmelo Meadow near kiosk

zigzagging left and right down more, you'll see Point Lobos' south-ernmost *Gibson Beach* , which marks the southern boundary. Stay on the trail curving (right) through the brush and you will come to the junction with the *Bird Island Trail*. Turn right and make your way along a cliff overlooking the emerald-green water of *China Cove*.

Bird Island Trail descends a long set of crude steps to the reserve's south parking lot. Skirt the left side of the lot, heading slightly downhill, to pick up the trail near where the road enters. Wind your way along the *South Shore Trail*, which hugs the shoreline to your left. It zigzags through brush for a few hundred yards. Keep the paved road to your right and avoid any spur trails that lead to the rocky beaches. A section of the trail makes a prominent horseshoe bend around a small rocky cove. Beyond this bend you come to a sandstone conglomerate shelf that creates a significant hump in the trail. Run up and over it, watching your footing. Just past this hump is the junction with the *Mound Meadow Trail*, where you continue ahead along the *South Shore Trail*, roughly tracing the irregular coastline northwest .

As you now run toward the sea on a small point (don't go all the way out to the end), look for a set of crude steps that turn downhill to the right. After descending these steps, you level off at an open area with a number of little intersecting trails. Stay on the obvious main trail northwest where it runs only a few feet above a beach with two names—*Pebbly Beach* and/or *Weston Beach*. Along this section the trail skirts the paved road.

You soon come to a spot where the trail dumps you into the road for a few feet. Cross the dirt car pullout, pass a water faucet, and pick up the trail just beyond. Continue on the windy shore-hugging route to another pullout. Run through it along the seaward edge to a steep set of steps at the north end. You drop down into a rocky trough and immediately pick up another steep set of steps going up to your right. At the top of this second set you level off, heading toward the great *Sand Hill* leg burner!

Actually, the *Sand Hill* is not what it used to be before steps were installed. You used to have to run up a sandy trail that made you feel like you were slipping back one step for every two steps forward. Now there are many crudely fashioned steps that allow the runner to take this hill with far less effort. Nevertheless, it's still a workout!

At the top of the steps a trail comes in from the right. Head left, out and around the point, which rises high above numerous coves. At the next junction, turn right and run the *Sea Lion Point Trail* to a large, paved parking lot. Angle across it to your left. Pick up the trail beginning just left of a display case. Though you start out on the *Cypress Grove Trail*, you're only on it for a few feet before turning right onto the *North Shore Trail*.

In 50 yards you pass the *Old Veteran Trail* to your left. Keep straight ahead and begin a long left-curving climb up crude steps under beautiful cypress trees. At the top of these steps you reach a junction with the *Whalers Knoll Trail* coming in from the right. Continue ahead, immediately dropping to cruise beneath the knoll. After 200 yards you reach the top of a long set of crude steps that curve to the left. At the bottom is a treacherous rocky area that you must cross to reach the trail continuation beyond it. A wrong step here could mean a very bad fall.

Once past this rocky ledge, go a short distance to a junction under the outstretched limbs of cypress trees. Turn right and immediately begin climbing granite steps. For the next 200 yards the trail undulates radically over rocks, roots, and steps—obstacles and potential pitfalls for the inattentive. The views, if you dare to deflect attention from the rugged trail, are fantastic through this section.

Just past a set of steep crude steps that descend to the left, you climb briefly to a junction (left is the root mass of a large overturned pine). Rather than turning right here to climb *Whalers Knoll*, you keep straight ahead. This section is rocky and rooty, so watch your footing; also, all left turns here lead to dead ends. Beyond a bench you make a right turn through a very rocky area. You have to negotiate an even trickier rocky section for the next 100 yards to reach a junction with the *Cabin Trail*. Turn right. (If you miss this turn you'll end up at *Cannery Point* with all the tourists!)

Recently rerouted, the *Cabin Trail* no longer drops down via a set of steps to a paved road. The new and longer trail descends behind the *Whalers Cabin*—offering better views of *Whalers Cove*—before joining the road. Turn right onto the road and get over to its left side, just above the beach. Almost immediately you angle off left onto the trail bordering a large meadow above the beach. This area offers a nice reprieve from the tricky footing required on the hills. At the next junction, turn right (south) on the newly rerouted (formerly named) *Carmelo Meadow Trail* to reach the kiosk.

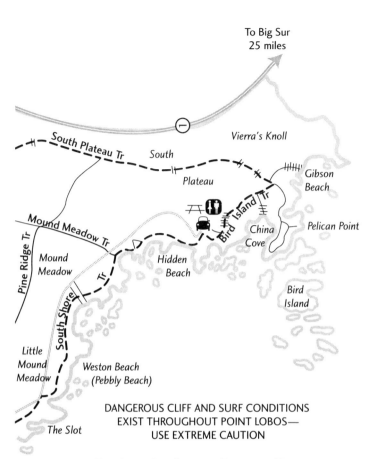

To Big Sur
25 miles

South Plateau Tr

South

Plateau

Vierra's Knoll

Gibson
Beach

Bird Island Tr

China
Cove

Pelican Point

Mound Meadow Tr

Pine Ridge Tr

Mound
Meadow

Hidden
Beach

Bird
Island

South Shore Tr

Little
Mound
Meadow

Weston Beach
(Pebbly Beach)

The Slot

DANGEROUS CLIFF AND SURF CONDITIONS
EXIST THROUGHOUT POINT LOBOS—
USE EXTREME CAUTION

Point Lobos State Reserve

Run 14

Big Outer Loop

Big Outer Loop

Distance: 6 miles   Difficulty: 👟👟👟

This grand tour of Point Lobos puts together the best parts of all the other runs here. You will know you've had a workout when you've finished this route but you'll want to do it over and over again.

Just beyond the entrance kiosk you will see your trailhead to the left (south). For the first 100 yards on the *South Plateau Trail* you run levelly or on a slight upgrade. Next, the trail winds and climbs moderately steeply for another 100 yards, before beginning a long, windy downhill. Be careful not to trip over the network of tree roots that protrude above the ground. Where the trail levels off, you reach a junction with the *Pine Ridge Trail*.

You continue straight ahead, cross a short split-log footbridge, and begin a short, steep climb over a small rise. Your downhill stretch is longer than the ascent in this direction. Below the rise the trail levels off and winds through pines for 100 yards. Then, after a long moderate climb topping out at a large pine (left), the trail descends a brushy south-facing slope. Descending a first set of crude steps and zigzagging left and right down more, you'll see Point Lobos' southernmost *Gibson Beach* , which marks the southern boundary. Stay on the trail curving (right) through the brush and you will come to the junction with the *Bird Island Trail*. Turn right and make your way along a cliff overlooking the emerald-green water of *China Cove*.

Bird Island Trail descends a long set of crude steps to the reserve's south parking lot. Skirt the left side of the lot, heading slightly downhill, to pick up the trail near where the road enters. Wind your way along the *South Shore Trail*, which hugs the shoreline to your left. It zigzags through brush for a few hundred yards. Keep the paved road to your right and avoid any spur trails that lead to the rocky beaches. A section of the trail makes a prominent horseshoe bend around a small rocky cove. Beyond this bend you come to a sandstone conglomerate shelf that creates a significant hump in the trail. Run up and over it, watching your footing. Just past this hump is the junction with the *Mound Meadow Trail*, where you continue ahead along the *South Shore Trail*, roughly tracing the irregular coastline northwest .

As you now run toward the sea on a small point (don't go all the way out to the end), look for a set of crude steps that turn downhill to the right. After descending these steps, you level off at an open area with a number of little intersecting trails. Stay on the obvious main trail northwest where it runs only a few feet above a beach with two names—*Pebbly Beach* and/or *Weston Beach*. Along this section the trail skirts the paved road.

You soon come to a spot where the trail dumps you into the road for a few feet. Cross the dirt car pullout, pass a water faucet, and pick up the trail just beyond. Continue on the windy shore-hugging route to another pullout. Run through it along the seaward edge to a steep set of steps at the north end. You drop down into a rocky trough and immediately pick up another steep set of steps going up to your right. At the top of this second set you level off, heading toward the great *Sand Hill* leg burner!

Actually, the *Sand Hill* is not what it used to be before steps were installed. You used to have to run up a sandy trail that made you feel like you were slipping back one step for every two steps forward. Now there are many crudely fashioned steps that allow the runner to take this hill with far less effort. Nevertheless, it's still a workout!

At the top of the steps a trail comes in from the right. Head left, out and around the point, which rises high above numerous coves. At the next junction, turn right and run the *Sea Lion Point Trail* to a large, paved parking lot. Angle across it to your left. Pick up the trail beginning just left of a display case. For this route you keep straight ahead on the *Cypress Grove Trail*, ignoring the right turnoff for the *North Shore Trail*, all the way out and around the point.

Along the *Cypress Grove Trail* you make a loop (in either direction) around the lovely *Allan Memorial Grove* of cypress trees. This

Sand Hill steps at Point Lobos

otherwise beautiful and easy section does have some tricky footing over a rocky area at the farthest end of the point. Because this is also one of the heaviest visited sections of Point Lobos, you'll want to time your run carefully to avoid the crowds.

Having closed the loop and retraced your steps almost as far as the parking lot, take a sharp left turn onto the *North Shore Trail*. In 50 yards you pass the *Old Veteran Trail* to your left. Keep straight ahead and begin a long left-curving climb up crude steps under beautiful cypress trees. At the top of these steps you reach a junction with the *Whalers Knoll Trail*, where you turn right.

You begin an immediate and gruelling climb along switchbacks to the top of *Whalers Knoll*. Watch your footing as you run through this summit area because the trail is quarried right out of a granite shelf. After a gentle ascent the downhill stretch begins. Bearing left where the trail snakes around some thick pine trees will let you descend at an easier incline. Keep left at the junction where an alternative route from the pass (in *Run 11*) joins your route. The trail curves left under a large, leaning pine, and then sharply right along a switchback. Monarch butterflies roost in the pines in winter along this downhill stretch. If you dare to take your eyes off the tricky trail underfoot, look down the hillside for views of beautiful coves far below. At the next junction (just below the pass), turn left and continue steeply descending to a junction with the *North Shore Trail*, marked by the large overturned pine. Turn right.

This section of the *North Shore Trail* is rocky and rooty, so watch your footing; also, all left turns here lead to dead ends. Beyond a bench you make a right turn through a very rocky area. You have to negotiate an even trickier rocky section for the next 100 yards to reach a junction with the *Cabin Trail*. Turn right. (If you miss this turn you'll end up at *Cannery Point* with all the tourists!) Recently rerouted, the *Cabin Trail* no longer drops down via a set of steps to a paved road. The new and longer trail descends behind the *Whalers Cabin* where it offers better views of *Whalers Cove* before joining the road.

Turn right onto the road and get over to its left side, just above the beach. Almost immediately you angle off left onto the trail bordering large Carmelo Meadow above the beach. This area offers a nice reprieve from the tricky footing required on the hills. At the next junction (right) with the formerly named *Carmelo Meadow Trail*, continue ahead on the *Granite Point Trail*.

The *Granite Point Trail* winds in and out of the woods offering occasional views of *Whalers Cove*. You run along a cliff at one point where you can look down to its crescent-shaped, dark sand beach. Then you drop into a section of trail pleasingly canopied with flowering shrubs. Slow down here because just beyond is a trail junction to your left. Turn left to circle *Coal Chute Point*, which affords fantastic views of coast wildlife. Circle this point in either direction; either way you get some short but steep, uphill switchbacks.

After completing this circle you continue left on the *Granite Point Trail*. Your route is relatively flat for the next 200 yards, but then you descend a flight of crude steps to a junction. A right turn here

Cypress Grove Point at Point Lobos

would take you out across a wide-open area to the northern boundary of Point Lobos. A sharp left turn would take you down to a rocky beach known as *The Pit*. But another set of crude steps lies directly opposite. Take them to begin a curving climb up to *Granite Point*.

There are some potential false turns along this section, where there appear to be trail junctions, but the attentive runner will easily find the main trail. After 100 uphill yards through brush cover, you come to a junction. Make a loop of *Granite Point* in either direction. Be careful: there are plenty of places to trip over protruding rocks and take a nasty spill. You circle this point around and beneath a prominent granite monolith at its center. After completing this loop head back the way you came, once again circling *Coal Chute Point*, perhaps now in the other direction.

Retrace your steps on the *Granite Point Trail* to the junction with the rerouted (formerly named) *Carmelo Meadow Trail*. Turn left. You gradually ascend through a forested area for a few hundred yards before several hundred flat yards ending at the kiosk.

"
Don't feel guilty about missing a run. Once that mind-set takes over, your joy of running diminishes—then the mental energy required to keep running exceeds the physical energy it takes to get down the trail. "

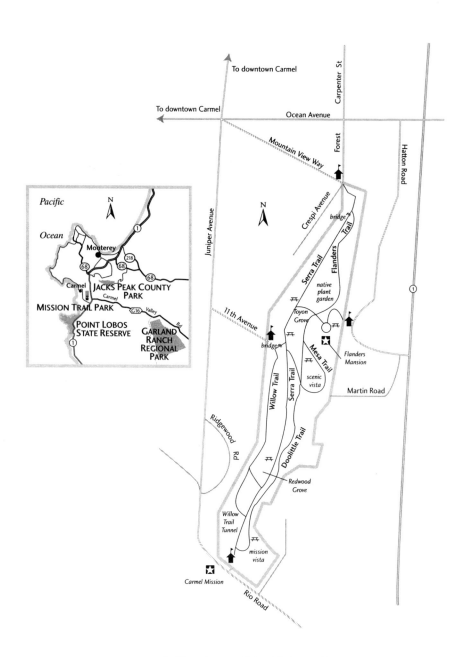

Mission Trail Park

Mission Trail Park

THIS DELIGHTFUL LITTLE CANYON PARK, SIT-
UATED RIGHT IN THE MIDDLE OF CARMEL,
HAS ONLY THREE MAIN PARALLEL TRAILS RUN-
ning its long, skinny north-south orientation,
yet the runs' range of difficulty and possible
distances allow you to get some very good
workouts.

You can choose to run at the bottom of
the canyon, alongside a seasonal creek and
beneath a forest canopy, or you can choose
the route that climbs above, affording views of
the Carmel Mission and the coastal mountains beyond.

I have encountered a variety of wildlife in
the Mission Trail Park. Bobcat, owl, hawk, fox,
cougar, and a variety of snakes either inhabit
or traverse this canyon park domain.

"Listen to your body. There's an important difference between discomfort and pain. The old axiom that suggests "no pain, no gain" can result in injuries that derail your running for weeks or months."

Arched footbridge at Mission Trail Park

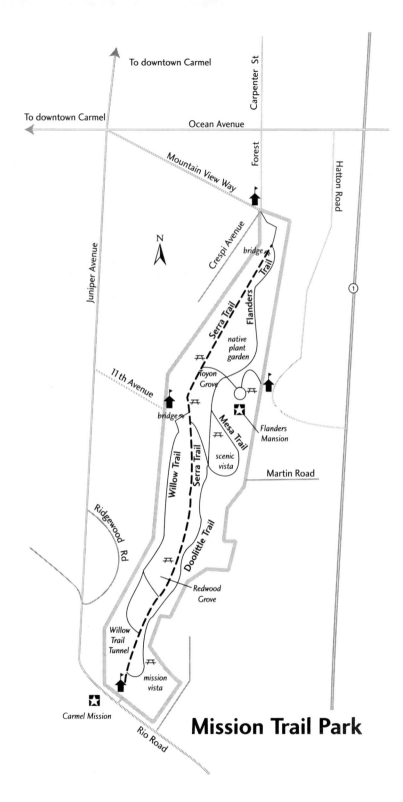

To downtown Carmel

To downtown Carmel

Carpenter St

Ocean Avenue

Forest

Hatton Road

Mountain View Way

Juniper Avenue

Crespi Avenue

N

1

bridge

Serra Trail

Flanders Trail

native plant garden

11th Avenue

Toyon Grove

bridge

Flanders Mansion

Willow Trail

Serra Trail

Mesa Trail

scenic vista

Martin Road

Ridgewood Rd

Doolittle Trail

Redwood Grove

Willow Trail Tunnel

mission vista

Carmel Mission

Rio Road

Mission Trail Park

Lower Gate to Upper Bridge (& back)

Distance: 1.4 miles   Difficulty: 👟

This is probably the least interesting route in the Mission Trail Park, but it's still quite attractive. From the Rio Road gate across from the Carmel Mission, your route simply follows a fire road, which is officially named the *Serra Trail*.

The first quarter mile is flat and all dirt. The road's bedding changes just past the concrete trough that channels the seasonal creek around the small meadow. After crossing this trough the road is surfaced with a thick layer of wood chips, which tend to float away during the rainy season, leaving the route quite boggy.

Stay on the wood-chipped road as it winds gently uphill for its entire length. The road ends at a narrow footbridge, where you turn around to begin the long downhill cruise back to the entrance gate.

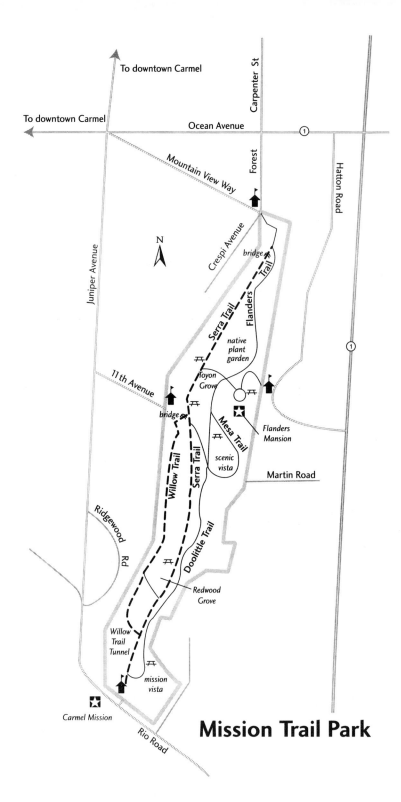

To downtown Carmel

To downtown Carmel

Carpenter St

Ocean Avenue

Forest

Hatton Road

Mountain View Way

Crespi Avenue

N

Juniper Avenue

bridge

Flanders Trail

Serra Trail

native plant garden

11th Avenue

Toyon Grove

bridge

Flanders Mansion

Mesa Trail

Willow Trail

Serra Trail

scenic vista

Martin Road

Ridgewood Rd

Doolittle Trail

Redwood Grove

Willow Trail Tunnel

mission vista

Carmel Mission

Rio Road

Mission Trail Park

Upper Bridge (& back) via Willow Trail

Distance: 1.4 miles   Difficulty: 👟

This route adds variety but not distance to the straightforward fire road (*Serra Trail*) described in *Run 15*.

From the entrance gate on Rio Road run along the dirt fire road for 200 yards to the second left-branching trail junction—this one obvious and officially designated the *Willow Trail*. Angle off to your left.

You are now running over a thick carpet of wood chips. The trail undulates over uneven ground for almost a half mile before curving right toward an arc-shaped footbridge. Cross this first bridge and then immediately reach another one. Beyond the second and larger bridge is a junction with the main fire road. Turn left and stay on the *Serra Trail* as it climbs to the footbridge at the top end.

From the bridge you either return to the entrance gate as you came or stay on the fire road. This route's variation makes it more interesting than the previous one.

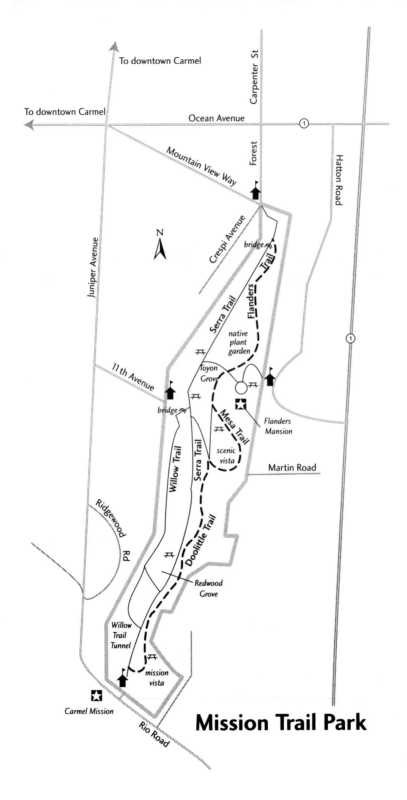

To downtown Carmel

To downtown Carmel

Carpenter St

Ocean Avenue

1

Forest

Hatton Road

Mountain View Way

1

Crespi Avenue

Juniper Avenue

N

bridge

Flanders Trail

Serra Trail

native plant garden

11th Avenue

Toyon Grove

Flanders Mansion

bridge

Mesa Trail

Willow Trail

Serra Trail

scenic vista

Martin Road

Ridgewood Rd

Doolittle Trail

Redwood Grove

Willow Trail Tunnel

mission vista

Carmel Mission

Rio Road

Mission Trail Park

Eastside Switchback Route

Distance: 2 miles   Difficulty: 👟👟

This longest run in the Mission Trail Park is my favorite route here. Besides some hard uphills, interesting switchbacks, and fine views, it offers you little likelihood of encountering other people. I typically run this route and back from 3 to 4 times, giving me a very hard 6–8 mile workout.

Inside the entrance gate on Rio Road, and to the right of the main fire road, you will see a sign for the *Doolittle Trail*. Take this trail and within a 100 feet you have to leap across a deep trough. After this jump you climb uphill, curving left across a hillside, where you get good views of the Carmel Mission and the coastal mountains to the south.

The first segment of the *Doolittle Trail* ends after a quarter mile at the concrete trough, which channels the seasonal creek around the small meadow. You run briefly on the main fire road, which you reach by bearing slightly left and then straight ahead. At the fire road turn right; you come to a bench and a trash can within 100 feet or so. The continuation of the *Doolittle Trail* goes sharply uphill from the right just beyond the bench.

The trail now climbs to a single switchback. After another short uphill you descend to traverse above but parallel to the fire road. Bear right at connector trails to avoid dropping to the fire road. To the right of another bench, turn sharply onto the *Mesa Trail*, which

89

Switchbacks in Mission Trail Park

climbs a set of five switchbacks. At the top of this set you have earned a flat cruise across the mesa, where you will pass another bench.

Beyond this high bench the trail drops steeply, passing a junction with a trail that comes in from the left and then descending to another junction where a trail comes straight up toward you. Here you turn right and begin an immediate steep climb. At the top of the climb you cross a short, log bridge. Just past this bridge is a Y-junction, which gives you a choice.

Either take the very steep right fork or continue straight ahead. Although both connect to a branch fire road leading uphill to a botanical reserve and historical house called the *Flanders Mansion*, the right fork will take you directly to the trail's continuation across from the fire road. Because the straight trail requires you turn right at the fire road and run uphill for a short distance to reach the route's continuation (left), I always take the steep route going uphill and save the other for the return leg.

The route continuation across the branch road is called the *Flanders Trail*. Along it you continue a steep climb to a junction that comes in from the right. Curve to the left here and immediately find a short, level stretch for a (partial) recovery. Soon the trail climbs gently to another junction. Again, curve left. This route finally tops out under some young oaks. The trail gently roller-coasters for another 100 yards and then—just as you pass a large, tabletop tree stump to the left—you descend steeply to the upper footbridge, the turnaround for all routes in this park. Return the way you came (or choose one of the other runs back).

Afterword

THERE ARE FAR MORE THAN 17 TRAIL RUNS IN THE GREATER MON-
TEREY PENINSULA AREA AND I'M SURE THAT MANY OF YOU know
OTHER ROUTES YOU ENJOY RUNNING. THE ROUTES I'VE INCLUDED IN
this guide are not only my favorites; they also represent a significant
amount of time and distance that I have spent traveling them.

Keep in mind that any of these loop routes, run in the opposite
direction, will give you a completely different run and perspective.
Strenuous uphill stretches one way become empowering downhills
the other. And you get different views! By adding up the possible
runs, you'll find enough for a different one every day of the month.
Once you become familiar with all the routes in a given locale, get
creative by linking runs or segments together, making new routes that
add variety and challenge.

Acknowledgments

THOUGH THE INSPIRATION FOR THIS GUIDE AND ALL OF THE LEGWORK TO COMPILE DATA IS SOLELY MY OWN, THERE ARE THOSE whom I feel deserve some recognition for their friendship, inspiration, and supportive work.

First of all I'd like to recognize my friend, Jeffrey Paul Schaffer, guidebook author extraordinaire. Though I wrote the first edition of the runner's guide more than a decade prior to meeting Jeffrey in 1989, I had been a fan of his unequalled hiking guides since the mid-1970s. Jeffrey's renowned guidebooks cover such mountain and wilderness venues as Yosemite National Park, the High Sierra, the Ventana Wilderness, and the entire Pacific Crest Trail, as well as many others. Since meeting him and becoming friends, I've been involved to a limited extent in Jeffrey's "earth-shaking" geological research and theories regarding glaciation and uplift of the Sierra Nevada range. Jeffrey has been generous in acknowledging my contributions for two of his books: the newest edition of his famous hiking guide for Yosemite; and his monumental treatise on glaciation/uplift titled *The Geomorphic Evolution of the*

Yosemite Valley and Sierra Nevada Landscapes. His guidebooks and his brilliant insights into the nature of nature have served to keep me inspired.

In 1979 I met Joe Henderson, former editor of *Runner's World* magazine, at a book-signing party in Pacific Grove following a 10K race in which I had competed. I told Joe that I had recently authored a runner's guide for the Monterey Peninsula. He asked me how many trail routes were in my guide compared to the number of paved routes. When I told him it was about 50-50, he suggested that I delete the paved runs and focus solely upon all the wonderful trails this area has to offer. At the time I thought I needed to fill my guide with over three dozen routes that catered to "street runners" as well as trail runners. It's taken over 20 years to realize that pounding pavement is not where it's at for me. I have no idea if Joe Henderson is alive or dead today, but I'm giving him recognition for his shared love of trail running.

I would be remiss if I were to forget the late Gamble brothers, John and Bob. These quirky fellows shared a passion for nature photography; together they captured Point Lobos' beauty in shots that continue to adorn postcards and calendars. Often during my runs there I would see the Gamble brothers wearing their photographer vests and wide-brimmed hats, standing behind their cameras and tripods. They were both well into their eighties when they died, and remained creatively active right up to the ends of their fascinating lives.

For the various maps I've copied for use in my guide, I want to thank designers working under these auspices: the City of Carmel-by-the-Sea, Point Lobos State Reserve, Monterey County Regional Park District, and Monterey County Parks System.

Finally, I want to thank my wife, Teresa, for the years we have spent running most of these trails. Our shared passion for running in the solitude of the woods was a key factor in us coming together in 1983. Indeed, our love of one of this guide's venues, Point Lobos State Reserve, led us to select it as our wedding site in 1985. Teresa's assistance in word processing has helped immeasurably in getting this guide completed.

—*Jeffrey Van Middlebrook*

About the Author

JEFFREY VAN MIDDLEBROOK HAS BEEN RUN-
NING SINCE 1965. WHETHER OR NOT HE HAS
COMPLETED THE EQUIVALENT OF A CIRCUM-
navigation of the earth in mileage, he has cer-
tainly logged what amounts to three, coast-to-
coast round trips of the United States on the
Monterey Peninsula alone, which should
make him the leading "expert" on trail running here. In his "obsessed," competitive
youth he set a personal record in the 10K distance of 32:49, and one in the marathon distance of 2:42:00. He was the first local runner
to envision and publicly suggest a Big Sur
marathon in the mid-1970s, when he was a
member of a local running club. In November
of 1976 he completed a grueling, solo, 65-mile
loop through the Ventana Wilderness in 14
hours, sunrise to sunset—no support team or
aid stations, just running clothes, a stash of
candy bars, and a water bottle! When not
working "in the field," he lives with his wife
and four children in Pacific Grove, California.

Index

Allan Memorial Grove, 75
author's favorite runs, 15, 27

bathroom, 19, 32, 36
BBQ and picnic areas, 19, 28, 32, 36
benches, 15, 16, 60, 64, 89
best runs, 15, 27
Big Outer Loop, 74
Bird Island Trail, 63, 69, 74
birds, 55
Buckeye Trail, 41, 45
burn-out, vii

Cabin Trail, 71, 77
Cannery Point, 71, 77
Carmel, 2, 81
Carmel Mission, 81, 85, 89
Carmel River, 39, 41, 42
Carmel Valley, 28, 32, 36, 39, 46
Carmel Valley Road, 3-4
Carmelo Meadow, 69
Carmelo Meadow Trail, 55, 71, 78
Ceanothus Trail, 32, 36
China Cove, 69, 74
Coal Chute Point, 55, *56*, 77, 78

Coffeeberry Trail, 15
Cottonwood Trail, 42, 46, 47
cougars, 11, 23, 39, 81
Cypress Grove Loop, 7
Cypress Grove Trail, 70, 75
cypresses, 75-76

Del Monte Forest, 2
dangers on trails, 11-12
deer, 20
difficulty of runs, 1
Doolittle Trail, 89

Earl Moser Trail, 19, 28, 32, 36
Eastwood, Clint, 20
fees for park entrance, 3

Fern Trail, 45, 46
Fife, Hugh Benjamin, 16
fire hydrants, 32, 36

fire roads, 23, 28, 32, 35, 36, 85, 87, 89
Flanders Mansion, 90
floodplain, 41-42
fog, 6

Garland Ranch Park, 3-4, 7, 8, 38-47
Garzas Canyon Trail, 46
Gibson Beach, 69, 74
Great Inner Loop, 31
Great Outer Loop, 35
Granite Point, 56, 78
Granite Point Trail, 55, 77

Iris Trail, 32, 37

Jacks Peak, *ii*, 3-4, 7, 8, 10-37

Lace Lichen Trail, 59, 64
laps, 15

Madrone Trail, 32, 36
Maple Canyon Trail, 45
maps, 1, 4, 15
Mesa Trail, 41, 45, 46, 89
Mission Trail Park, 4-5, 80-91
Monarch butterflies, 60, 77
Monterey Bay Aquarium, 50
Monterey Bay, views of, 11, 15
Monterey pine, 7, 16
Monterey-Salinas Transit (MST), 5
Mound Meadow Trail, 53, 59, 64, 70, 75
mountain lions. *See* cougars

natural dangers, 7-8, 11-12
North Shore Trail, 61, 70, 75, 76, 77

Old Veteran Trail, 70, 76
Olmsted Road, 3

Pacific Grove, 2
parking lots, 31
pavement, impact on body, vii3

pay phones, 27, 31
Pebble Beach, 2
Pebbly Beach, 70, 75
pepper spray, 12
philosophy of running, vii
Pine Ridge Trail, 51, 53, 59, 63-64, 68, 74
Pine Trail, 28, 36
Point Lobos State Reserve, 4, 6, 7, 15, 48-79
public transportation, 5

Rio Road, 5, 85, 87, 89
Rhus Trail, 32, 36, 37

Sage Trail, 45
Sand Hill, 70, 75
Sea Lion Point Trail, 70, 75
Serra Trail, 85, 87
Sky Trail, 46
Skyline Trail, 37
snakes, 81
Snivley's Ridge, 45, 46
South Plateau Trail, 53, 68, 74
South Shore Trail, 64, 69, 70, 75
Sycamore Trail, 42, 46, 47

The Pit, 56, 78
tourists, 6, 50, 59, 68, 71, 77
trees, 7-8, 32, 50, 53, 63, 75, 78

views, 11, 15, 28, 42, 81, 92
visitor centers, 41, 45, 47

Waterfall Trail, 46
weather and seasonal conditions, 6-8, 39
Weston Beach, 70, 75
Whalers Cabin, 71, 77
Whalers Cove, 55, 71, 77
Whalers Knoll, 59-61, 71, 77
Whalers Knoll Trail, 70, 76
wildlife, 55, 77, 81. *See also* cougars
Willow Trail, 87
women, safety issues for, 12